MW01092685

IAN FLEMING'S
SEVEN DEADLIER SINS
& 007'S
MORAL COMPASS

A BIBLE STUDY WITH JAMES BOND by
BENJAMIN PRATT

For ongoing discussion and additional material, visit

www.BondBibleStudy.info

Published By:

Read The Spirit Books

an imprint of
David Crumm Media, LLC
42015 Ford Rd., Suite 234
Canton, Michigan
USA

For information about customized editions, bulk purchases or permissions contact:

David Crumm Media, LLC at 734-786-3815

Dedication

In gratitude and loving memory
of the man
Who taught me to
Read the Spirit
beneath the words,

The Reverend Harry M. Taylor, Ph. D.

Professor of
Classical Literature and Preaching,
Wesley Theological Seminary,
1959–1974

Please Note …

This guidebook to unlocking the spiritual themes in James Bond is designed for both individual enjoyment and group discussion—so a Study Guide and supplemental materials to help with discussions appear at the end of the book.

If you're planning a group discussion, invite individual members of the group to pick up various Bond books and let those individual members become your group "experts" on the novels. It's a fun idea and will add to the vitality of your reflections.

CONTENTS

PREFACE

I n the early 1960s, I had just turned 10 when I overheard my Methodist aunts discussing with obvious disapproval that my dashing Uncle Warner "seems to enjoy those James Bond movies" and had taken my equally dashing Aunt Helen to see *Dr. No* and now *Goldfinger*, as well.

I adored both my Uncle Warner and my Aunt Helen—the closest thing I could envision in my huge family to Hollywood-style celebrities. Warner was the troubled son of what passed for wealthy aristocracy in northern Indiana. Helen was the most beautiful of the immigrant, Swiss-American Yunker sisters. She was swept off her feet by Warner. A military officer, Warner served in India during World War II and Japan after the war, where the two of them began rearing their children. When they finally moved back home to Indiana, they brought back exotic Asian furniture and spread out their holdings inside a stately brick home on what seemed to me to be a grand estate with horses and miles of glistening white fence.

Warner wrote poetry, sometimes deliberately provocative poetry— the only man in my family I knew who pursued such an eccentric art. He was a not-always-recovering alcoholic and remarkable storyteller who kept me riveted to the dinner table with the adults even long after the dessert dishes were cleared. He had secrets.

Even as a child, I could tell that by just looking into his face with that thin Clark Gable moustache, elegantly placed cigarette and broad-brimmed fedora whenever he went out. He read voraciously. I recall sneaking into his grand office one day to discover a row of Ian Fleming novels, which at age 10 were a daring treat. I immediately sprawled on the rug as the afternoon sun beaming through tall windows moved across the floor and finally faded into dusk as I lost myself in James Bond's adventures.

This was an exceedingly mysterious world—a frightening, delicious realm of deadly drama that took my breath away as a child. I could scarcely fathom what I was reading, but I kept reading novel after novel. Of course, my reading, too, was a dark secret. I vividly recall my aunts' disdain for Fleming, whom they called "junky," as damning a verdict as strict Indiana Methodists could muster in that era. I vividly recall one of my aunts, after discussing the women and guns in the Bond movies in politely euphemistic terms, concluding, "Well, Warner's the kind who would like that."

In awe, I wondered: What "kind" is that?

Now, literary scholar and retired pastoral counselor Benjamin Pratt has unlocked an entire chapter of my life that I dimly understood. In the course of this book, you'll discover that Ian Fleming himself was a troubled son of the aristocracy who wound up in military service and, despite deep emotional troubles throughout his life, was drawn like a magnet to contemplate the timeless spiritual forces at work in this modern world of self-destructive temptations. He was a deliberately provocative writer whose approach to the literary arts earned damning reviews from the elite far beyond the leading Methodist circles in the American Midwest.

No, this book is not some scholar's attempt to force an ill-fitting spiritual interpretation over the top of a body of literary work. Benjamin Pratt has spent years researching Ian Fleming's life and especially Fleming's fascination with various modes of understanding the "deadly sins" in our world. Over the years, Pratt has written many articles, talks and manuscripts about Fleming's spiritual themes. He has lectured widely on the subject and, now, has written a new kind of Bible-study guidebook to exploring Fleming's themes, as relevant today as they were in the heart of the Cold War.

This book is written with the highest respect for Fleming's work and it would please all of us immensely if we played a catalytic role in helping more readers to discover the books first published half a century ago by this writer whose literary skills frequently are disdained by critics and observers like my aunts. In fact, this book encourages group study participants to go out and buy a lot of Fleming's novels—using an unusual group format in which each group participant reads a different Bond book and becomes a resident "expert" on a particular book. With Pratt in one hand and a Bond novel in the other, you'll have an eye-opening and heart-opening couple of months!

What a delicious idea, hmmm? After all these years, Ian Fleming finally breaks into those church circles that once shuddered at his revelations. Perhaps his still-fresh spiritual reflections will wind up electrifying Bible-study groups that may be languishing after too many years' diet of traditional Biblical curricula.

As a journalist specializing for decades in exploring the impact of religion on the world, I love Pratt's approach to unlocking dark secrets about our world and our own lives. You will read, in the course of this book, not only his analysis of what Fleming really is trying to tell us—but you'll also read passages written by men and women in various forms of government service, talking about how many of these themes are very close to home.

That's why I can say I am rediscovering my most romantic and mysterious uncle in working with Pratt to publish this guide to Bible study with James Bond. My own mother, Helen's youngest sister, frequently told me as a child, "If you didn't live through the war years in the '40s, you just can't understand how they were."

I was still a child when Warner died. I recall asking my mother, in the midst of the mourning process, what it meant to be an "alcoholic," a term I had overheard that was new to me. And, to her line about the war years, my mother added, "I don't think you'll ever understand your Uncle Warner. He was a very good man, a great man really. But I don't think you'll ever understand him."

Half a century later, thanks to Benjamin Pratt, I think I'm beginning to understand my uncle a little better. That's the promise within this book: You may discover something important about yourself or people close to you as you explore these pages.

—*David Crumm, Founding Editor*, ReadTheSpirit.com

INTRODUCTION
ON THE CENTENARY OF
IAN LANCASTER FLEMING
(MAY 28, 1908, TO AUGUST 12, 1964)

Ian Fleming was born 100 years ago and died at the youthful age of 56, before millions of his fans were even born. But Fleming's creation, James Bond, Agent 007 of the British secret service, appears to have no end. He is licensed to kill in an incredibly lethal profession, yet has been endowed by his fans with an eternal life of danger and intrigue, moving through exotic cultures, bedding beautiful women and enjoying fine food and drink in striking locales.

"Bond, James Bond." Around the world, these three words summon visions of adventure that strain credulity. Bond movies have grossed billions over the past 40 years. *Casino Royale* (2006) alone was nearing a worldwide gross of $600 million at the time of Fleming's 100th birthday. The 22nd Bond film, *Quantum of Solace*, débuts in November, 2008.

Together, Fleming and Bond have reshaped how movies are staged, crafted and marketed. Much of the current perception of the James Bond character—sexually irresistible, dangerous, debonair, socially astute, heroic, clear of purpose and always prepared for the action-packed life—is based on the film genre. However, only two of the films were released in Fleming's lifetime. Even those films reflect the strong influence of producers Albert R. "Cubby" Broccoli and

Harry Saltzman, director Terence Young and scriptwriter Richard Maibaum.

The Bond books are a media milestone all their own. By 1965, the year following Fleming's death, nearly 60 million copies of his 007 books—starting with his first, *Casino Royale*, in 1953—had been sold in 18 languages. Through the years and the countless impressions of the Bond myth stamped in billions of minds around the world, however, the epic themes of novels and films have diverged.

To truly understand the spiritual core of the modern world's most famous spy, we have to return to Fleming's original novels. Fleming wrote 12 novels and two collections of short stories about Bond. And within these 14 books lies a surprisingly different theme than the global image of the mythic secret agent today.

All of Fleming's 007 tales follow a common theme that he identified in *Casino Royale* as parables about evil people. This revival of Fleming's original themes is a tribute to his creative and spiritual vision. Some critics have dismissed Fleming as a literary lightweight—or condemned him for "sex, sadism and snobbery."

In the book you are about to read, you will discover that Fleming's stories have considerable mythological, allegorical and theological depth deserving this revival. In fact, Fleming's James Bond opus (the 14 books as a whole) was the first contemporary narrative treatment of a centuries-old spiritual concept: the Deadly Sins. Today, nearly half a century after Fleming's death, the "Deadly Sins" have jumped back into our common cultural conversation around the world. Nearly 4 million Web sites in 2008 touch upon the "Deadly Sins." And this is not surprising.

We live in a time when evil, quite literally, falls out of the sky. "Evil" is a fitting word to describe the events of September 11, 2001, when civilian airliners were hijacked as lethal projectiles to destroy the altars of our cultural gods. The World Trade Center, as the economic symbol, and the Pentagon, as the military icon, were devastatingly struck. One hijacked missile, surely aimed at our altars of democracy, the White House or the Capitol, was commandeered by heroic civilians and crashed into a Pennsylvania field.

We live in a time when evil takes many forms. Many ethical business people labor long hours in our global economy today, but we also seem to have nests of unethical competitors who cook the books of avaricious major corporations, making them appear to be far more profitable than in fact they are. When these truths come to light, sometimes thousands of persons lose jobs and retirement savings, while the CEOs of these corporations often glide to earth on golden parachutes.

We live in an era when we rightly remember the Holocaust with horror. We regularly commit ourselves as communities and nations to creating a level playing field for all people regardless of faith, culture or origin. Yet we stand aside, quietly kicking the pebbles beneath our feet with eyes averted as new genocides unfold in distant lands. Are we powerless to act?

We live in a time when human cruelty and malice are staples of news media. While we universally condemn such acts, there is something about these evils that fascinates us. Hollywood and the digital gaming industry know that ever more ingenious and realistic ways of depicting cruelty and malice sell their products. Are we as addicted to violence as we are to oil?

We live in a time of moral ambiguity amidst wars and rumors of wars.

We live in an era that Ian Fleming glimpsed and instinctively saw the need to probe in prophetic ways.

Good reader, you may be weary of this catalog of human evil. I understand that temptation to withdraw. It is easy "to grow weary in well-doing." I know that from experience. It happened to me. I burned out as a pastor. Lost my zest for the work I had been called to do. And when that happened, I lost a part of me. I nearly lost my marriage. The downhill slide from courageous engagement with life is often subtle. But left unchecked, its destination is sure: a certain loss of faith in the goodness of life, leaving us dry, bitter, full of dust—empty of life.

If you've experienced such a spiritual season in your life—well, you're in good company. For, you see, *James Bond also burned out*! And the only cure for his condition was for M to send him on an impossible mission: to ferret out an evil dragon.

If you're burning out—and even if you're not—I have an impossible mission for you: find a way, in your own life, to join James Bond, Agent 007, in slaying the dragons of Moral Cowardice, Snobbery, Avarice, Hypocrisy, Cruelty, Malice, and Self-Righteousness. If you do, the evil dragon of burnout, which Ian Fleming clearly understood and referred to as "Accidie", will vanish.

Oh, yes. One more thing.

Don't be seduced into believing that evil lurks only in the hearts of the Hitlers, the Darth Vaders, the Goldfingers, the dictators of the world. Fleming knew that the dragons of evil have their habitation within your heart and mine as well. We'd rather stay comfortable and look only at other people's evil. But we need also to confront our own as James Bond was called to do in each of Fleming's tales. Otherwise, evil will triumph. If you do choose to honestly work your way through this book, you are making a courageous choice to struggle with the darkness in your own soul and the soul of our world.

Beyond this personal and corporate darkness, we yearn to rediscover the light and hope in the heart of God. In this first decade of the third millennium of Christianity, the most potent charge laid before Christians is this: we have failed to come to grips with evil in our modern world.

The point I'll be making in this book is that the author of the biblical *Letter of James,* as well as Ian Fleming himself, set pen to paper as a challenge to all of us to battle evil—whether it be found in high places or in ourselves.

In our present age, the world's 2 billion Christians, long associated with centers of power in the West, certainly are front and center in Fleming's spiritual re-evaluation. But this book represents a fascinating journey whatever your faith may be—or even if you have no religious affiliation at all.

So come along as we explore together *Ian Fleming's Seven Deadlier Sins and 007's Moral Compass.*

CHAPTER 000
OUR MORAL COMPASS
CRACKING THE 007 CODE

James, a bond servant.
—James 1:1 KJV

A man may say, "You have faith and I have works: Show me thy faith without thy works, and I will show thee my faith by my works."
—James 2:18 KJV

O Prince! O Chief of many throned pow'rs!
That led th' embattl'd seraphim to war.
—John Milton

Put on the whole armor of God,
that ye may be able to stand against the wiles of the devil.
For we wrestle not against flesh and blood, but
against principalities, against powers,
against the rulers of the darkness of this world,
against spiritual wickedness in high places.
—Ephesians 6: 11-12 KJV

If you are not facing down Demons – you're not truly alive.
—Maya Angelou

M y pilgrimage in cracking the 007 Code sometimes felt as though I was caught up in the pages of a novel.

In August, 2000, I was bicycling for ten days around Lake Champlain in northern Vermont. One unseasonably cool evening in a small clapboard motel tucked back from the highway amidst birch and pine trees, I did what I often do when I am alone in such a setting. I reached for the Gideon's Bible, which lay alone in the small drawer of the pine bedside table. I flipped through the pages of this well-worn book with a scuffed blue cover to a short letter, called the *Epistle of James*. I was startled to the point of shaking when I read the opening words:

"James, a bond servant…" *(James 1:1)*

Sleep was not restful that night, nor was riding properly balanced the next day. I had come here with two couples to get away from the mental stresses of my life, to push and test my muscles, to soak up the beauty of nature, to drink a little beer, eat good food and laugh with good friends. I am a former pastor who has spent my life chasing links between the spiritual and the profane. This journey to Vermont was to have been a little oasis—not a life-changing confrontation with one of my greatest quarries: the Bond of fiction and the Bond of moral and spiritual reflection. Yet there lay the words on this little page in this out-of-the-way inn: "James, a bond servant…"

My mind raced: Could there be any connection? Why had I not seen this before? I knew that Felix Leiter, Bond's CIA sidekick, referred to 007 as "St. James" on more than one occasion. I knew that each time James Bond writes a letter to his demanding, puritanical boss, usually with the intent of resigning, he signs it: "I am, Sir, Your Obedient Servant." I knew that a "bond servant" is one who serves under command, laboring for another.

I sat, pondering this reference. In biblical studies, we know that references to slaves and servants are difficult for modern readers to understand. In the New Testament, all slaves are servants, but not all servants are slaves. "Servant" also can be used to describe the adherent of a chosen deity, ruler or agent—like M in the Ian Fleming novels. "Servant" also describes the nature and resilient loyalty of James Bond, a man branded, like a slave, with an inverted "M" on the back of his right hand.

So many associations surfaced that evening. I knew that many commentators on the Bond literary tales have called them profoundly Christian, very male and quite sexist. I knew that the *Epistle of James* only mentions the name of Jesus twice and is more an ethical compass than a theological treatise. I knew that James Bond's faith is in fact expressed by his works, which is the core assertion of the Epistle: "…I will show thee my faith by my works." *(James 2:18)*

My gut more than my head told me that here, sitting with a scruffy little Gideon's Bible in my palm amidst pine and birch, I had found a pattern that would weave together threads I had collected over many years of researching Fleming's work and legacy. It never fails to astonish me how I can ride a bicycle with total awareness of my terrain and at the same time be deeply absorbed in filtering the threads of intellectual and emotional research and emerge not only safe but rejuvenated because of the interface of the two exercises— the physical and the intellectual. I had been so eager for this retreat in Vermont but now wanted nothing more than to return to my basement study where I could attempt weaving a full fabric of Fleming's spiritual message.

When I got home the following week, I had barely kissed my wife before I was overwhelming her with a flood of words about my trip and my Gideon discovery. Soon, I was drawn down to my study and my old oak desk, once a fixture in a government office but eventually discarded by the feds. It's perfectly at home in my study, encased with knotty pine bookshelves filled with novels whose authors have befriended, challenged, comforted and perplexed me. To my left are my shelves filled with Bibles and books on faith. Among these shelves are all of my well-marked, tattered Signet paperbacks of the James Bond tales, Fleming biographies and commentaries—and a related collection of books on the nature of good and evil.

I immediately turned to my collection of Bibles. Thinking I could quickly find the translation I sought, I turned to a volume that contains 26 translations of the New Testament. "James, a bond servant" was not listed as a translation. I leafed through other Bibles including one published in London in 1854—only to be again disappointed. My balloon of excitement was deflating and I felt bewildered but not completely deterred.

I decided that more important than finding a Bible with a translation like the one I had read in the Gideon's Bible was to determine if there was any link between "James, a bond servant" and Ian Fleming. This meant turning to Fleming's personal collection of books.

In 1929, Fleming began a friendship that would last his lifetime with an astute bibliophile, Percy Muir. In 1934, under Muir's diligence and mentorship, Fleming began the acquisition of a first edition collection of the crucial books "that started something and made things happen." These books were responsible for the exceptional technical and intellectual transformation of the world since 1800. By the time the collection was complete it contained printed sources on great inventions, discoveries and scientific theories of the modern times—as well as minor, but valuable treatises. The books and papers included aeronautical theory, wave theory, nuclear theory and germ theory of disease to name only a few. His collection included a rare early copy of Marx's *Communist Manifesto* and Hitler's *Mein Kampf*, Darwin's *Origin of the Species*, and first editions of Freud. Each of Fleming's volumes on science and philosophy was in its original language. Near the end of the acquisitions, Muir and Fleming sought to collect the significant literary figures of the period as well. This collection of first editions responsible for the modern revolution became so valuable that it was housed for safety by Oxford during the Second World War.

In 1968, four years after Ian Fleming's death, his wife Ann sold his entire collection, including the original hand-edited James Bond manuscripts plus all of his other personal books to Indiana University in Bloomington, Indiana. Included in this exceptional collection, now housed at the Lilly Library on the campus of Indiana University, is Fleming's personal Bible.

I emailed Christopher Harter, my contact at the Lilly Library, with a description of my request as follows:

Among your Fleming collection is his personal Bible. It is a King James Version of the Bible. Some of the KJV Bibles are slightly different than others. I am particularly interested in the *Letter of James* in the New Testament. In some KJ Versions that I have found it begins: "James, a bond servant…" I am curious to know if the particular version you have in the collection begins with this language. I think that Fleming may have gotten his idea for the James Bond character from this source. I know that the dominant theory is that he took the name of an American ornithologist, James Bond, and used his name. But, Fleming was fond of and trained in the creation of hoaxes. His 1939 paper "Rumour As Weapon" and his task often as the creator and executor of "hoaxes" on the Nazis was among his favorite work.

Would you be willing to look at the Bible, the Letter of James, and let me know how the version in the Fleming collection reads?

Mr. Harter's response is as follows:

Fleming's copy of the KJV Bible begins, "James, a servant of God…" with 'servant' footnoted. The footnote reads, "Gr. Bond—servant"; the Gr refers to the Greek text from which the KJV was translated. I hope this helps in your research.

Help and hope were realized. My balloon was re-inflated with hope and a basis for my next step of inquiry.

My Adventurous Life in Bondage

My adventures with Bond stretch over so many years that I cannot recall which perilous challenge we faced together in our maiden voyage. I do vividly recall that Bond always was interrupting even my most cherished holidays from the pressures of my work as a pastoral counselor on Capitol Hill and in Northern Virginia. For some reason, the tension of skiing down a slope with bullets flying around me or sloshing through the rat infested sewers of Istanbul was always a relief—compared with the anxieties of tracking through the muck and mire on Capitol Hill.

I first found myself hanging from a cliff with 007 on a family vacation in southwest Virginia, at a surprisingly delicious retreat called Hungry Mother State Park. When not feeding worms to fish that never took the hook, or frolicking in the cold mountain lake with our children, or eating and laughing ourselves silly with our dearest family friends, I found time to escape with the only Bond book I owned. Almost certainly, a half-clad woman and a gun graced the cover. I do remember that I had the first tale finished within two days and was off to the used bookstore where I found three others that surely were a sign of my new addiction.

In each of my adventures with James Bond, whether sitting on pine needles at the edge of a mountain lake or in my hammock in my back yard, Fleming was enticing me away from the pressures of my daily life to join Bond in the violent struggles between the cosmic forces of light and darkness. Without moving a muscle from my world, Bond was inviting me to engage and grapple with good and evil.

These are mythic narratives. More than that, they are astonishing theological parables.

One keyhole through which I glimpsed that truth is a seven-letter word derived from Greek. I was startled to discover that the word shows up in nearly every Fleming tale: accidie. Why does this word appear so often? It's usually well placed as a description of the motivation of the most evil opponents of Bond—as well as a description of 007 himself, when he is bored between the demands of his mission-driven life.

Accidie, it turns out, is one of the original seven deadly sins that was defined in the Middle Ages by its symptoms: sloth and torpor. Accidie comes from the Greek *akedos,* which refers to those who didn't care enough to bury the dead on the battlefield. Their energy and the dreams that energized them had been drained. Accidie defines the loss of the dream that gives our lives definition, meaning and passion. The disappointment of the loss of the dream can leave a person at the edge of despair. The loss of the dream saps us of our energy and joy and hope in life. It is a form of moral lassitude and spiritual suicide. The religious say that it even results in the loss of faith in the very goodness of God. But there it is! That unusual word—accidie—one of the original deadly sins—is laced throughout the Bond tales.

And, from that key, the further I searched in the Bond adventures, I began to see other deadly sins—and finally, as amazing as it may sound even as you read it in these pages—all seven were there—elegantly portrayed in the characters and eloquently described in their speeches, even more so than they were defined in earlier narrative treatises by such giants as Chaucer, Spencer, Langland and Dante.

I became convinced that this was intentional on the part of Bond's scribe, Ian Lancaster Fleming. As my research unfolded over the years, Fleming seemed to be the first modern author—in fact, the first author in centuries—to write narrative tales expressly personifying deadly sins. Fleming carefully built Bond's larger-than-life tales in which the very future of the world rests on Bond's battle-scarred shoulders—on the foundations of an ancient architecture. These are struggles not so much with lasers and guns, cars and criminals—but with timeless temptations that lure each of us each day.

A crucial link in the chain of my early discoveries occurred while researching for my doctorate in the dusty library shelves of Wesley Theological Seminary. I stumbled across a small volume called *The Seven Deadly Sins*, published in 1962. The Foreword was written by Ian Fleming. I opened it with as much delight and startling surprise as I did the Gideon's Bible years later.

Fleming begins his Foreword in *The Seven Deadly Sins* by declaring that the idea for the series of articles contained in this small volume was presented by him while on the editorial board of the Sunday Times in London. He also reveals that it was he who arranged to publish the series of essays by different authors, mainly by authors he suggested, on the traditional seven deadly sins: Pride, Envy, Anger, Sloth (Accidie), Covetousness, Gluttony and Lust. It is important to note that this little book, *The Seven Deadly Sins*, was published one year after Ian Fleming's first heart attack. Fleming never fully recovered from this attack but, in spite of his frailty, continued to write as if his life work and mission were more important than life and comfort. He persevered with his writing until his death following a second attack in 1964. Fleming, in spite of his success, never felt he had been truly acknowledged for the quality of his literary output. The Foreword to *The Seven Deadly Sins* provides a substantial clue to a rarely acknowledged motive in his creation of the James Bond tales.

In a bold statement in this Foreword, Fleming turns the traditional seven deadly sins on their heads by proclaiming they are closer to virtues than the sins he observes in our time. He even proceeds to describe the ancient sins as virtues of the specific persons who had written each of the essays. For example, he praised the Pride of Dame Edith Sitwell and the Covetousness of Cyril Connolly. He compared Gluttony with the tremendous zest for life of Patrick Leigh-Fermor. And Lust? Fleming hoped that he and Christopher Sykes would long remain lustful in their lives.

Fleming argues that most of these ancient sins will no longer keep one out of Heaven—except for one especially troubling sin: accidie. For Fleming, accidie or sloth could never be considered a virtue. Fleming, who was plagued with black, slothful moods all his life, believed that accidie, a form of spiritual suicide and a refusal of joy, deserved his complete denunciation because he had known its despair so often. So, except for accidie, Fleming finds most of the traditional seven deadly sins to be closer to virtues in our time, and to be the very spice necessary for the masterpieces of Shakespeare, Voltaire, Balzac, Dostoevsky and Tolstoy.

The essays in *The Seven Deadly Sins* deal with the traditional list, which had been enumerated by monks for monks within a monastery. So, in his Foreword to the book that collected these essays, Fleming provocatively suggests seven modern, deadlier sins, a remarkable idea that he carried into his cycle with Bond. Here is how Fleming enumerates the modern sins that definitely will lead to Hell: Avarice, Cruelty, Snobbery, Hypocrisy, Self-righteousness, Moral Cowardice and Malice. Fleming voiced his hope that someone of equal caliber to the seven essayists in the little volume he was introducing would go on to write about his list or perhaps propose their own list of deadlier sins.

The challenge was so tempting, in fact, that Fleming accepted it himself! In the Bond tales, in spite of mentioning the original seven deadly sins, his primary focus is on his deadlier seven, plus accidie. He personifies each of the deadlier sins in the evil characters Bond pursues as well as in Bond himself.

And here is where the 007 code twists, turns and reconnects us with the biblical record—because when I compared Fleming's list of deadlier sins with the *Letter of James*, even more strands wove neatly into place. At this point, here are three examples: avarice, hypocrisy, snobbery. Consider several passages from James:

The Letter of James 5:1-6 on Avarice

1: Go to now, you rich men, weep and howl for your miseries that shall come upon you.

2: Your riches are corrupted, and your garments are moth eaten.

3: Your gold and silver is cankered; and the rust of them shall be a witness against you, and shall eat your flesh as it were fire. You have heaped treasure together for the last days.

4: Behold the hire of the labourers who have reaped down your fields, which is of you kept back by fraud, crieth: and the cries of them which have reaped are entered into the ears of the Lord of sabaoth.

5: You have lived in pleasure on the earth, and been wanton; you have nourished your hearts, as in a day of slaughter.

6: You have condemned and killed the just; and he doth not resist you.

The Letter of James 3: 17 on Hypocrisy

17: But the wisdom that is from above is first pure, then peaceable, gentle, and easy to be entreated, full of mercy and good fruits, without partiality, and without hypocrisy.

The Letter of James 2:1-4 on Snobbery

1: My brethren, have not the faith of our Lord Jesus Christ, the Lord of glory, with respect of persons.

2: For if there come unto your assembly a man with a gold ring, in goodly apparel, and there come in also a poor man in vile raiment;

3: And you have respect to him that weareth the gay clothing, and say unto him, Sit thou here in a good place; and say to the poor, Stand thou there, or sit here under my footstool:

4: Are you not then partial in yourselves, and are become judges of evil thoughts?

These are sins that concerned the modern James—and the ancient, biblical James as well! As I raced through these comparisons between Fleming's canon of sins and what I believe was likely his biblical source—as the British would say, "I was gob smacked!" In my original research into Fleming, my interest in his exploration of sins was all built upon careful reading of his novels. Now, these connections were reinforced in surprising ways. I had been convinced, for instance, that *Casino Royale* provided clues to the entire series, but the weaving together of Fleming's Foreword along with the identical ethical injunctions in the *Letter of James*, capped, sealed and confirmed my assumptions.

Casino Royale: Encountering the Nature of Evil

"The Nature of Evil," this four-word invitation into the spiritual odyssey that would unfold in Fleming's novels from 1953 to 1966, appears atop a chapter in the very first Bond tale, *Casino Royale*.

In this first of Fleming's 14 parables of evil, Bond faces Le Chiffre (The Cypher), an evil agent of the Soviet empire who has gotten himself into trouble by siphoning off money from his bosses and losing it in a grandiose scheme to operate brothels. The dramatic showdown at a glittering casino between Le Chiffre and Bond appears to involve cards and gambling chips, but really is a life-and-death battle for survival. If Bond wins, Le Chiffre will wind up deeply enmeshed in the debts he has accumulated and likely will be assassinated by his Soviet bosses. However, at one point in the novel, Bond winds up in Le Chiffre's clutches, taken as a captive into a devil's lair, Les Noctambules (the nightwalkers). In scenes of revolting cruelty Bond is punished by Le Chiffre, who taunts Bond in the voice of a punishing father, telling him that he has moved from childish games to the adult reality of cruelty and evil.

Bond, delirious with pain and near death, is saved by the most unexpected intervention: a Soviet SMERSH agent who kills Le Chiffre and spares Bond. In Fleming's tales, SMERSH (an actual division of the KGB) is a conjunction of two Russian words, *smyert shpionam*, which means "death to spies." This counterintelligence agency is committed to the assassination of Soviet traitors and double agents. Oddly enough, we find that there is a kind of honor among these Soviet skunks. Since Le Chiffre's killer has no order to terminate Bond, he is spared but his right hand is branded with a Russian letter resembling an inverted "M" to mark him as a spy in any future encounters. So Bond is not rescued by the British, the French, or the Americans—but by his Cold War enemies, the Russians, who step forward to crush their own traitors. The moral confusion of life is placed before us in narrative form. The devils of the Cold War appear miraculously to save an angel.

In the chapter called "The Nature of Evil," Bond is recovering in a hospital bed from Le Chiffre's torture and surprisingly engages in a philosophical-theological monologue with a French colleague. Bond waxes eloquently on the extremes of good and evil and their personifications as God and the Devil. He proclaims that we can clearly see the image of God and every hair of God's beard—but not the Devil. We don't truly know what the Devil looks like, says Bond.

Fleming, through Bond, is raising the question: So, what does the Devil look like?

This is the difficult question that Fleming seeks to answer in his twelve novels and two collections of short stories. Fleming essentially is writing a Devil's Bible. He invites us on a pilgrimage through parables, folktales, myths and allegories to show us not only what the Devil looks like, but also to define the motivations of evil. Bond says as much in "The Nature of Evil." He argues that, while there is a Good Book, the Bible, to define clearly the nature of goodness, there have been no prophets to write an Evil Book that would enable us to see the Devil clearly and define evil in its many forms.

In this spiritual quest, Fleming was drawing on a subject he knew all too well. He had observed Stalinism as a British journalist in Moscow prior to World War II. Later, as personal secretary to the Director of Royal Naval Intelligence, he saw first-hand the evils of Nazism. In addition to the horrors of evil he saw on both fronts, Fleming's father was killed in World War I, when Ian was not yet 9; his brother, Michael, was killed in World War II.

He was not alone among 20th Century writers pondering the moral confusion of industrialized warfare. C.S. Lewis, at one point, was left for dead on a WWI battlefield; Kurt Vonnegut was a prisoner in a meat locker called Slaughter House Five in Dresden, Germany, during the British fire-bombing of the city; George Orwell was shot through the throat in the Spanish Civil War; William Golding spent six years in combat with the Royal Navy; J.R.R. Tolkien served at the Somme in 1916. Each writer was drawn back, again and again, to contemplate the nature and contour of evil, expressing it in fictionalized tales.

Sending a New Knight Into the Fray

As Ian Fleming took his turn at this literary challenge, he created a man at war, but not a soldier. He created a knight—a modern personification of St. George, the dragon slayer. In his modern twist on the mythic knight, Fleming created a hero who often falters, fails to keep a constant vigil and finds himself captured by the dragons he pursues. Many of his battles are fought within his own soul. Many regard him as a scoundrel, a wily womanizer. Others view him as a symbol of courage, bravery, loyalty and devotion to the cause of the weak. He is a complex sinner who often acts as a saint. Fleming is asking us to consider: Can good and evil be embodied in one and the same person?

James Bond is a modern St. George. Fleming calls him that in eleven of the fourteen adventures. Shortly before his death, Fleming said it again—calling Bond a current-day St. George who kills wicked dragons. So, who was this mythic figure? Your answer depends upon which historical source you encounter, but he is esteemed enough to be honored by churches and countries on April 23rd. He is the Patron Saint of England. Some see him as a saint; others see St. George as a scoundrel.

The man often thought of as St. George, historically, was an archbishop of Alexandria, murdered by a mob in 303. Some historians saw him as a nasty figure who rose to power by fawning on his superiors in disgusting ways. He made a great deal of money from a defense contract to the army by supplying bacon. By manipulation he became an archbishop and was noted for plundering pagan temples and then taxing pagans and Christians beyond their endurance. He was arrested by a new administration and imprisoned for 24 days until an enraged mob could wait no longer. They bashed in the prison door and murdered him, carrying his body in an exultant procession through the streets of Alexandria and dumping his corpse in the sea. Another change of administration brought back his remains and elevated him to martyrdom and sainthood. Ah, the good old days.

There are other, more admirable accounts of the historical George, but it is the legend of St. George that is most important for our purposes. The legend is that a young knight came upon a grieving town where the fairest maiden had been absconded by a dragon. To the rescue came the young knight who traversed the horrors of fire, pestilence and snakes to kill the dragon and save the fair maiden and the people of the village. *Our Hero!* James Bond's faithful scribe, Ian Fleming, carefully retold this heroic tale over and over again, but nowhere more clearly than in *Dr. No*, in which we even encounter a fire-breathing mechanical dragon and the gauntlet leading to a Giant Squid. Our Hero!

So St. George must be reckoned with not only as a historical figure with less than sterling reputation (similar to 007), but also as a chivalric dream of England for centuries. And not only England has lifted battle cries in honor of St. George. He is the guardian saint of Sicily, Aragon, Valencia, Genoa, Barcelona, and Malta. There are chivalric orders also in his honor in Spain, Italy, Austria, Germany and Russia. Whoever he was, a shameful manipulator or a heroic savior, St. George has come to represent bravery by the strong on behalf of the weak, a patron of those who risk their lives in honorable struggles with a steadfast and brave heart—much like our Bond … James Bond.

What dragons was Bond sent to slay? In the Bond thrillers, another clue to Fleming's code is that there are other agents—008 and 0011, which coincide with the number of deadly sins in other codes devised down through the centuries. But, Bond was 007 with a license to slay, I am convinced, Fleming's Seven Deadlier Sins. In fact, Bond's foes are such fascinating, brilliant figures that they often are more interesting than Bond himself—much like our fascination with the imagery of the fearsome dragons, rather than St. George, in iconic images of the saint.

Fleming's modern twist is that, in addition to confronting the Devil in these seven deadly forms, Bond must confront the same evils in himself.

Fleming's Art of Deception

Often dismissed as a literary lightweight, Fleming is emerging as a complex figure. Again, he is not alone in this kind of reappraisal. Tolkien rose from the relative obscurity of a cult following in the 1950s until, by the turn of the millennium, some literary scholars were arguing that his *Lord of the Rings* was the greatest work of fiction of the 20th Century.

There are many signs that Fleming, like Bond, was a multi-layered figure, a man well acquainted with deception. In 1960, Fleming was a dinner guest at the home of John F. Kennedy as the young senator was planning his run for the presidency. When the conversation turned to foreign policy and how to deal with Fidel Castro, Fleming suggested that the Central Intelligence Agency should drop leaflets in Cuba announcing that beards are magnets that attract radioactive material, making men impotent. Such a trick would destroy the bearded leader's credibility and undermine his hold on the Caribbean island, Fleming suggested. A CIA operative who was present at the Georgetown dinner party knew that a variety of hoaxes designed to undermine the Cuban dictator were actually under consideration by the agency. Fascinated with Fleming's creative approach, he reported on the Georgetown dinner party to CIA Director Allen Dulles, who attempted to contact Fleming the next morning. But the writer already was on his way back to London.

The use of deception and hoaxes as part of warfare was an integral part of Fleming's work in his capacity as personal assistant to Admiral John Godfrey, Director of Naval Intelligence, and to Godfrey's successor for the duration of World War II. The scope of his war work was varied and demanding, and he was considered a valued and gifted servant. His training and experience in the office and as a representative of the Naval Intelligence Division around the world provided vast material and expertise for this future writer.

In July 1939, shortly after becoming Godfrey's secretary, Fleming wrote a paper called *Rumour as a Weapon*. He wound up playing a small part in the development of one of the Navy's most elaborate and famous deceptions, known as The Man Who Never Was. Fleming's admiralty-office colleague, Commander Ewen Montague, brilliantly executed this hoax. The body of a British sailor was washed up on a Spanish shore, carrying highly valuable operational information about an impending Allied invasion in the eastern Mediterranean. When the Germans found the body, they believed the information and moved their forces to defend against a non-attack.

Fleming, trained in such sleight of hand, naturally toyed with readers in his Bond novels. That's why I'm not convinced by the conjectures that the hero's name refers to "Bond Street" in

London—or to the ornithologist James Bond, who wrote a 1947 Field Guide to Birds of the West Indies, a book displayed on a table at Goldeneye, Fleming's writing retreat in Jamaica. When viewed in the context of all fourteen tales, the name and character of James Bond fits "James a bond servant" from the *Letter of James* more closely than the other possible sources. Surely, Fleming's sleight of hand would have carefully chosen his hero's name to fit his purpose. Since Fleming gives such obviously symbolic names to other characters, could we expect him to have done less with his hero?

The *Letter of James*, written in a time of war when the early church defined itself as under a constant threat from the forces of evil, only mentions the name of Jesus twice. The letter is a practical guide that focuses on the actions of faith. "Show me how anyone can have faith without actions. I will show you my faith by my actions," it says. Just as the author of the *Letter of James* witnessed to the practical actions of faith as well as the limitations and sinfulness of the faithful, so our hero James Bond embodies both the actions of faith and the sins of the faithful.

I Have Seen the Enemy—In the Mirror

I accept the fact that Ian Fleming was a troubled soul. I accept the fact that he may have taken to flights of fantasy to deal with his internal pain. I know that he was a loner, had poor relationships with women whom he seduced and abandoned. He may well have been sadistic and cavalier.

I accept that he was insecure, deeply anxious, felt unloved and undervalued, lived in the shadow of his successful elder brother, fell short of his nearly sanctified father who died on the battlefield of World War I when Ian was almost nine, lived in the tension of his love/hate dependency on his emotionally distant mother all his life. Do I think all this played out in his writing? Of course, I do. But I do not hold Fleming in contempt for his condition. I accept that he was a troubled and wounded soul who experienced his inner life as a battlefield on which his Scottish puritanical roots were at war with his prideful, anxious, licentious, freedom-yearning spirit. It is the spiritual battle and the struggle with evil that raged within Ian

Fleming that is writ large in the parabolic novels we know as the James Bond series.

Every creative work reflects the life-long autobiographical journey of its author. The poet Rilke, a deeply disturbed man, quit therapy because of his fear that if he cured his devils, his angels would leave also. He knew that both were born of the same wounds and the attempts to heal those wounds. As a pastoral counselor myself, I have worked with many troubled persons who experience their souls as battlefields. I have come to love and admire them as persons of faith and courage who are seeking to keep their external lives and relationships from being destroyed by their inner struggles. Often they fail, as Fleming frequently failed in his struggle. But, like Fleming, many keep themselves in balance through an artistic, creative expression.

Confronting demons is a constant, lifelong spiritual battle for many. It was for Fleming. It is for me. It is for many people whom I have come to love and admire as I have shared their spiritual pilgrimage.

When T.S. Elliot was asked, "What is morality?" he answered this question in *The Love Song of J. Alfred Prufrock* by saying we need to walk through the streets looking and listening to the sounds and voices that cry out the soul's moral ache.

Ian Fleming responded to the question, "Who is the Devil and what is Evil?" To find the answer we must walk through the streets looking and listening to the sounds and voices that cry out our soul's moral ache. We must venture into smoke and sweat-filled gambling casinos that erode our souls, through castle courtyards of poisonous plants and pools of toxic liquids, through rat-infested sewers that lead to spy telescopes. We must walk the golf links of Kent, the beaches of Jamaica, the dimly lit streets of Turkey and the bleak streets of Harlem, Las Vegas and Miami. In half-deserted streets we see, hear, taste, touch and feel Fleming crying out to us.

Moral Inventory:

Now, it is time for you to act, perhaps even to cry out yourself. The following questions and suggested activities are designed to open this interaction, whether you are working alone or in a group. Throughout this book, I will invite you to return to this process in new ways. You may want to take a moment and read the Study Guide at the end of this book—or you may simply want to dive in right away.

Ponder, journal or discuss:

Think of a person who you think of as evil. Can you think of any good qualities also embodied in this person?

Think of the things you admire about your government—local, state, national. Now think of areas where you think each fails to govern well and justly.

Evil is conceived by the union of prideful loneliness and belligerent impotence. Evil is born a dragon with many heads and tails. Evil is nurtured and grows in the lonely illusion of prideful god-like power.

Think of a time when you interacted with another person in a way that seemed to help that person. Now think of a time when you interacted with another person in a way that in some way diminished or hurt them. What was at stake for you in each instance? How did you feel afterward? (Note: It is not at all clear that you would feel good after the first instance and bad after the second – so note your actual feelings.)

Draw or make some other artistic representation (music, acting) of you when you're feeling or acting as a good person. Draw or make some other artistic representation of you when you're feeling or acting evil.

Which of the following bothers you the most: moral cowardice, hypocrisy, self-righteousness, cruelty, malice, snobbery, avarice or accidie? Have you ever been victimized by such sins? Have you ever embodied these eight qualities?

After you complete this initial inventory, feel free to jump around in this book to chapters that intrigue you. The book can be read cover to cover—but you may find yourself drawn toward chapters in a different order.

CHAPTER 001
MORAL COWARDICE

*Blessed is the man that endureth temptation: for when he is
tried, he shall receive the crown of life, which the Lord hath
promised to them that love him.*

*Let no man say when he is tempted, I am tempted of God: for
God cannot be tempted with evil, neither tempteth he any man:
But every man is tempted, when he is drawn away of his own
lust, and enticed.*

*Then when lust hath conceived, it bringeth forth sin: and sin,
when it is finished, bringeth forth death.*

Do not err, my beloved brethren.

  —James 1: 12-16 KJV

For more than five years, until her death in 2006, I regularly
visited a wonderful woman whom I came to admire until
sparks of love and warmth flowed between us. She had been
reared in the inner city of Washington, DC, never married,
and taught English literature in Washington's public schools until
her retirement in her mid-sixties. Then she became a noted Bible
scholar and a much sought after speaker, especially in Episcopal
circles. When I entered her life she was in her mid-eighties,
confined to a wheel chair and finally to her bed, living her last days

in a retirement/nursing facility. It was in that nursing center that I visited Verna Dozier.

As a young woman, Verna and her father walked to the chapel at Howard University to worship and hear Howard Thurman preach. Howard Thurman, Dean of Howard University from 1936-1944, was a poet, author, philosopher, professor and preacher who crafted eloquent sermons for his congregation. In her final years, Verna could not often recall what had happened an hour ago, but she quoted poetry, hymns and occasionally the wisdom of her favorite poet, Howard Thurman. I clearly remember the warm, sunny day I had pushed her wheel chair onto a rooftop garden and she told me, eyes closed as she soaked in the warmth of sunshine, that Thurman said there are two basic questions in life: "What are you going to do?" and "Who are you going to travel with?" And then he had added, "Don't get them out of order."

Howard Thurman would say that I got my priorities out of order. Ian Fleming would say that my choice of family and love of my wife ahead of my primary mission in life was an act of moral cowardice. I lacked the moral courage to choose my mission (what I do) instead of my love life (with whom I travel).

I suspect that many of you are objecting to how I have just drawn such a clear dichotomy, especially since marriage is a life mission undertaken before God. Marriage is something that one *does*. Well, I understand that objection and I know that I have wrestled with this at times which has made these spheres of my life anything but a dichotomy. Our choice of partners and our sense of mission often mingle in muddy ways throughout life. But I am also clear that frequently, for me, these issues are very sharp and dualistic.

My approach to these issues I'm sure is rooted in my own childhood, when I learned that my mother became an invalid because I was born. At least, that is the way the story came to me and settled into my soul. As a child I watched her steady deterioration and believed it was because I was born. This created in me a deep sense of shame, a basic awareness that I am toxic and can hurt others. This, of course, is different than guilt, which is all about things that we *do*. Shame is about something we *are*.

My mission as a pastor was powerfully driven by the hope that I could do something that would justify my existence and thereby redeem my life from my own basic nature. In that, I think Ian Fleming, James Bond and I have something in common. Fleming lost his father early in life as did Bond, who lost both parents. Fleming found his greatest sense of purpose in his mission as personal secretary to the head of Naval Intelligence. Bond found his value in his exploits against evil demons. Each of us found meaning, even redemption, in our life mission—and often at a high cost for our loved ones with whom we travel.

In the 1960s I was a parish pastor working to found a new congregation twenty-five miles south of Washington, DC. In eight years I received more than 1,400 new members, provided oversight for the design and construction of a sanctuary and education building, founded a performing arts society, volunteered with the fire and rescue squad, served as an officer of the civic association and was considered successful in nearly every aspect of this wonderful and difficult work. I averaged 70-80 hours of work per week and, although I burned out badly, I loved the work. The pressures on my marital and family life were excessive and corrosive to those relationships. We came close to our marriage failing and were saved by my breaking both arms at the same time, which forced us back together, literally and confessionally. After extensive training I was offered a job as a pastoral counselor and I took it. It was less demanding time-wise and I was able to give myself to my wife and children more consistently than as a parish pastor. I grew to love my new work and my new approach to family life, but I lived many years after leaving the parish with the nagging sense that I failed my primary calling, my primary mission as a parish pastor.

Many rush to disagree with me about this. This certainly is not the way many people define the issue of moral courage or cowardice. But, if your worldview is defined by a calling to a larger sense of mission, duty or faith (as a bond servant), then this perspective on moral courage or moral cowardice is quite understandable. Such a worldview is basic to most people whose lives are defined and directed by their spiritual faith or religious duty—but it certainly is not limited to that sphere. You may have felt these particular pangs in your own work, let's say, as a teacher, a police officer, a fireman

(Read: *Last Man Down* by Richard Picciotto), an artist, a nurse or in a role in the military or government service. You've probably wrestled with this question on these terms—and you'll find this same perspective threaded throughout the James Bond tales.

Over the years, it has been my privilege to know agents in the FBI, DEA, Customs, CIA and Border Patrol. I decided to check out my interpretation of the moral courage/cowardice issue with a couple of friends. After all, James Bond is a government civil servant.

Here is how these agents responded to an early draft of this chapter you are reading right now. I'm not including their names here to protect their professional identities:

> Ben,
>
> Just finished your chapter on Moral Cowardice. I want to share a couple of thoughts in no particular order.
>
> 1. I liked the premise—think you hit on what is truly a fundamental struggle for anyone who is in the line of work which, as you state, is "defined by a calling to a larger sense of mission, duty or faith." How does one balance the mission, in Bond's case duty to country, with everything else? It is what keeps most of us up at night. It is what made coming home from Iraq when I knew others were still there so incredibly difficult.
>
> 2. I'm not convinced that this sense of duty "What are you going to do?" is necessarily mutually exclusive from "Who are you going to travel with?" Unequivocally there is a constant tension and at any given time one struggles to balance the two. Invariably one must give way to another. I would argue that one's priorities are constantly shifting as one travels through life. At times, work is a priority at the expense of friends and family. At times, vice versa. Someone once told me that it is less about what you do in life than about how you choose to do it. That seems cliché but the older I get, the truer it seems. At any given time we are neglecting something we cherish, value, and love. It is how we recognize, reconcile and rebuild that matters in the end.

3. What I am not sold on is whether choosing family/ friends/et al before the mission is a reflection of moral cowardice. I would argue that God gave us multiple gifts/ talents with the expectation that as well-rounded people we would be called upon to serve in many different ways— as a good case officer, a good daughter, son, friend, etc. I do not believe choosing one role, as a husband/father, over one as a case officer would reflect moral cowardice. I think it would depend more directly on the reason I made those choices and why I chose to stack my priorities as I did. If the intentions are pure—as was your case in choosing your family over your mission—God could not possibly find you or me lacking…

4. I do agree with your notion that after his experience with Vesper (in *Casino Royale*) Bond avoids any future entanglements and dedicates himself relentlessly to the job and the greater mission. However, I think that his various and sundry affairs, beyond a reflection of moral ambiguity, are frankly my definition of moral cowardice. Specifically, his unwillingness to commit again for fear of being hurt, begs the question whether his dedication of mission is really born of a sense of duty or simply his effort to escape another, more complex sense of responsibility on a more profound, personal level. Or perhaps, as you note, it is the embodiment of accidie. He seeks to fill that void continually with everything but a personal life. Frankly, in my experience on the job, the officers with well-rounded lives are the ones who are generally the most grounded because they have the most to lose. The ones you keep an eye on—the ones you worry about going rogue—are those who single-mindedly are consumed by the mission.

You've hit on an important topic that in this day and age we all struggle to get a handle on. I know I rarely feel that I am all that I should be and often wonder if I have made the right "morally courageous" choices. I suppose we will all ask ourselves that famous line in *Saving Private Ryan,* "Did we earn it?" Perhaps to answer that question we need to ask those whose lives we have touched the most—parents, siblings, children, etc.

Thanks for sharing with me. I enjoyed it and needless to say it stimulated a lot of thought.

Part of my response to this friend was:

What you have done is 1) ask the right questions; 2) push back in a balanced way; 3) push the issue to reflect a personal examination of your own life. You have taken my offering seriously and you have done the work I hope others will do in response to this journey with Bond and Fleming.

Another agent responded, in part, as follows:

When I first became an agent, I thought I was doing it for God, my country, my President and that my mission was tied to those ideals. My wife hated where we were assigned and I loved the work so much that I ignored her complaints—and often ignored her. I wanted to be at work even on my days off. I have learned some important things in recent years. I had to make some adjustments to balance my work and my family. Those who have not learned that are divorced … without their spouse and their children and generally in a lot of debt. The other important thing I learned is that we don't really tie our daily mission to the ideals of freedom or country or our President. In our scary and often life-threatening work, our primary mission is to our brothers and sisters who work along side each other in the field. We work to keep each other safe and out of harm's way as we carry out our mission/tasks. So, I have difficulty separating "what I do" from "who I travel with" because my primary loyalty is to the people I travel with in my work-mission as well as my family-mission.

Another agent and her spouse responded jointly with the following:

Hi Ben

I can very much identify with the "sense of duty" that some of your other readers (and Bond) share; however,

I don't think it's the result of holding a certain job or position. I believe that it is within the individual, no matter what vocation they choose, but it does seem that, more often than not, persons with this type of personality trait gravitate toward those jobs where the "sense of duty" or "mission" seems greater and thus perceived as more difficult to balance with personal goals and desires.

We have very different views on employment. While he gives 100 percent to his job, when on the job, when the bell rings, he believes his obligation and responsibility are over until the next day. Very rarely does a situation arise that keeps him after school or causes him to "bring his work home with him." I am sometimes envious of this ability, but it does make it very difficult to explain why I can't just pack up at 5:00 sharp and come home if the job isn't done; and I do believe that if he had a similar sense of commitment and/or duty, our personal struggles in this area would be lessened.

Sometimes because of these very differing viewpoints, it makes the choice easier when asking the question, "What will I do?" Right or wrong, good or bad, it is sometimes easier to stay at work with people who hold similar viewpoints and share that same sense of duty, than come home to tension, frustration, and disappointment when I have placed the mission ahead of the personal life. With a child, that decision has become a lot harder, because a child does not have the same cognitive skills to cope as an adult. The logical, fact-driven, mission-oriented side of my brain says my husband doesn't need the same attention and time that my child does because he's an adult. But the wife, mother, care-giver side of my brain says my family (whomever that is made up of) deserves my time equally, if not more, because without them, the journey ("What will you do?") doesn't mean as much. It's a constant struggle, but one that I think we will continue to endure, because our family is worth it—and when it stops being worth it, then the personal cost has been too great.

I too do not feel that the two (work life and personal life) should be mutually exclusive, but it is a careful balance, with many intricacies and pitfalls to successfully navigate. I see first-hand what happens to colleagues who go too far one way or the other. If they lean too far to the work life, they may lose their family (and perhaps part of themselves too) and too far the other way (not being vested in the work), which can result in not being thought of as a "good agent," a powerful fear for many agents.

My husband says that despite our differing views on commitment to the mission, he feels a sense of pride, and sometimes bragging rights, in telling people what I do. He also thinks he grounds me to some degree so I don't become someone who burns out at the job. He's right, to a degree, because I do think that, absent having my family, I could very well do just that.

I think the sense of mission/duty can be a convenient excuse to avoid dealing with some personal difficulties—and thereby be moral cowardice (and I think this is the case with Bond avoiding personal relationships in subsequent novels after Vesper's betrayal). Absent that, I don't think choosing "what you do" over "with whom you travel" is a reflection of moral cowardice. As I said, it's a constant struggle, both personally and with those with whom I travel—to balance the two and co-exist in a manner where I feel I am being true to my sense of mission and not sacrificing my personal goals/desires to satisfy that sense. While they are separate worlds (work and family), they are inextricably intertwined, which makes the questions, "What will you do?" and, "With whom will you travel?" difficult to separate.

Thank you for sharing your work with us. It has been quite thought-provoking and we look forward to more!!

As you read this book, today, if I can convince you to engage in these issues like these earlier readers, then I would have no hesitation in claiming that I have been faithful to my mission.

Myths, Parables and Allegories

Perhaps you're still at arm's length as a reader, however. There's no question that James Bond is an agent on a mission, but perhaps you don't think of yourself as an agent. Perhaps you've never stopped to sort out the relative values in your commitments toward your work and your family. Well, Fleming spun his tales on various levels, inviting readers to play with and rethink the novels' implications in fresh ways. Like many other writers, including popular religious writers, Fleming used myths, parables and allegories.

So, let's pause a moment to define this trio of literary devices.

A *myth* is a narrative used to clarify meaning when our normal reasoning cannot adequately explain the situation. Myth can make sense of a senseless world. Individual myths are stories that point in the direction of truths not adequately expressed in abstract language. Healthy myths are like safe containers for relieving excessive anxiety and neurotic guilt. For example, the story of Adam and Eve is a myth that contains the most basic truths about men and women and their fear, guilt, shame, frailty and limitations. This Adam and Eve myth—this grand, timeless story we share of first humans—acknowledges our relationship to a just and present God. In it, people know where they stand. They know their boundaries. They know their place. They know their journey. The best understandings of life are often contained in myths. This is true of God, the Devil, good and evil. Myths are powerful spiritual tools—revelations of truths so large that we could never fully glimpse them without a story we can grasp at the deepest level of our humanity.

A *parable* is a story that uses an oblique style to illustrate a profound truth. While history's best-known parables are those of Jesus in such stories as the *Good Samaritan (Gospel of Luke 10: 25-37)* or the *Prodigal Son (Gospel of Luke 15:11-32)*, the use of parables is not limited to ancient writings or religious literature. Parables are literary mirrors in which we are invited to make an inventory of our own spiritual and moral character. In parables, the story is one step removed from our own lives—so we can examine our own best and worst selves without too much anxiety. In a good parable, however, we may wind up with fresh insights into our own journey toward the heart of God and God's journey toward our hearts. We may even hear the voice of God calling us to repentance and forgiveness and new life with new values. But, of course, we are not always ready to give up our lives as we know them. In those instances, parables might wind up chilling us to the bone—or even drive us into indifference, blindness or stubborn impenitence.

A key distinction between parables and allegories is that parables invite us to explore a whole range of reflections from the basic story. At distinct times in our lives we may see our portrait reflected in different characters within a single parable. Think about the parable of the *Good Samaritan*. At many points in my life, I have been the Levite who passed by the injured man. I saw needs yet found reasons not to respond. But, at other times, I have responded warmly and was a reflection of the Good Samaritan in the parable. Of course, there also have been times in my life when I was the victim lying in the ditch!

In *allegory*, an author intends the characters and their actions to be understood usually in fairly specific terms. The writer of allegory usually weaves a series of symbols into a narrative to help us explore the underlying issues in a fresh way. C.S. Lewis's *The Chronicles of Narnia* often are described as the most popular allegorical novels in our era with the lion, Aslan, as a Christ-like figure. The novels invite us to think through Lewis's understanding of the gospels, and they are such an entertaining cycle of adventures that millions have read them. But allegory is a more specific window than either myth or parable. If myths and parables are reflective, allegory is geared more toward posing a provocative argument. In his Bond novels, Fleming frequently resorted to this technique, providing Bond with an arsenal of ideas with which to trick his enemies and even his readers. The Bond tales move so fast that it is easy to overlook deeper allegorical meanings that lie beneath the surface.

Fleming's Three Parables of Moral Cowardice: 1. Casino Royale

In many tales, James Bond is labeled a man of war. He is a man of duty, courage, perseverance and deep dedication to his assigned mission. As such, he is a bond servant. He is extremely loyal to M, his masterful director of the Secret Service, the British Intelligence Division of the Department of Defense. He is not a soldier, but James Bond is a man at war with nefarious criminals, the agents of the Devil. Bond is also a man of war confronting his own evil. This is the life-long spiritual war that unfolds in the battlefield of his soul. It is the eternal war of good versus evil. He confronts the dragons of evil that plague him personally as well as those personified by the evil characters he pursues. So, the James Bond tales are parables about the war waged against the noxious criminal elements of this earth, but they are also, secondly, a personal spiritual war against the forces of evil. The first type of war that Bond encounters is before him intermittently, but the second type of battle is always before him—and always before us, twenty-four seven.

Among Bond's personal delights is his attraction to women. As a man of war, the sirens who tempt this very eager lover confront him often with a moral dilemma: his mission or his lover, the crucial test of moral courage versus moral cowardice, especially for a man of war. In most of the tales of war, Bond is confronted by a delicious temptress who is usually quite beautiful, but often flawed: Vesper Lynd, Solitaire, Gala Brand, Tiffany Case, Tatiana Romanova, Honeychile Rider, Jill and Tilly Masterton, Pussy Galore, Domino Vitali, Vivienne Michel, Tracy Vicenzo Bond, Kissy Suzuki and, of course, Bond's secretaries, Loelia Ponsonby and Mary Goodnight.

Remember Thurman's two basic questions: "What are you going to do?" and "Who are you going to travel with?" These questions, and the admonition not to get them out of order, are pivotal in sorting out our relative courage or cowardice. In *Casino Royale,* moral cowardice appears as the central issue in the breakdown of Bond's relationship with Vesper Lynd. Bond, having been violently beaten by Le Chiffre, is nearly healed. He goes to a seaside resort with the beautiful and talented Vesper, a fellow secret service agent from

British Intelligence. He declares his love and proposes marriage. But the relationship begins to deteriorate as she becomes distant and secretive. Her evasiveness only becomes clear when we discover that she has been a double agent—and she commits suicide rather than meet the same fate as Le Chiffre. And, yes, Vesper's demise takes a different form in the novel than in the recent film version of this story.

In the novel, Bond kneels before the dead body of the woman he loves and weeps. The wall of mistrust that had been building between them had bewildered him, and he could not crack it. Now she is dead; her suicide note tells why. She became a double agent because, shortly after entering the Secret Service, she fell in love with a Polish member of the Royal Air Force. He, too, was trained by M and, as a British Secret Agent, was dropped behind enemy lines in Poland. He was captured by the KGB, who learned about Vesper by torturing him. The Russians contacted Vesper and forced her to work for them to preserve the life of her lover. Each month, she received a letter from her lover, verifying that he was still alive. She believed that she would be his killer if she did not continue to supply the KGB with information.

The suicide letter also gives details of her betrayals and clues for Bond to pursue the killers. His tears quickly give way to rage as he thinks of the agents who have been killed because she chose love over loyalty to the mission. The distressing moral ambiguity of the post-war world is captured in *Casino Royale,* and specifically in the bitterness of Bond's final remark about Vesper, who had seemed like an angel. Feeling betrayed and abandoned by her, Bond angrily spits out his rage at the dead "bitch." Fleming tells us much later in the series that Bond returned every year to Royale-les-Eaux to visit Vesper's grave. Perhaps he truly did love her. Perhaps the loss of this important lover contributed to Bond's refusal to consider marriage for many years, as well as committing him ever more intensely to his mission.

Moral ambiguity is a central theme of *Casino Royale.* Bond's battle with Le Chiffre confronted him early in the story with the same dilemma that confronted Vesper Lynd with her Polish lover. Le Chiffre kidnaps Vesper Lynd, who will serve as bait to lure 007 into a chase. Bond, who often is described as having cold, brutal eyes, especially when he is on duty, contemplates the dilemma as he races down the highway in pursuit of the kidnappers. He vows that he will not make an exchange for the girl. Because she was a member of the Secret Service, she knew the consequences, he reasons. The Mission is of greater value than the individual. Nevertheless, it is a terrible moral choice.

It is worthy of note that *Casino Royale* was written immediately following the scandalous defection from the British Secret Service by Guy Burgess and Donald Maclean, May 25, 1951. These two British agents, who had defected with atomic secrets to the Russians, were part of the "old boy" network, educated at Trinity College, Cambridge. This blemish on the British conscience and Service certainly was a true-to-life impetus for the moral dilemma integral to *Casino Royale*.

2. For Your Eyes Only

Even the meticulous guardian of morality, M, is confronted with a morally confusing dilemma, when he chooses to involve Bond in an act of personal revenge that pushes both of them outside their defined mission. *For Your Eyes Only* opens in the bucolic garden of the Jamaican plantation of Colonel and Mrs. Havelock, an aging couple who have respectfully cared for the land they love dearly. Mrs. Havelock is watching and feeding her streamer-tail or doctor hummingbirds. *Trochilus polytmus*, considered by many to be the most beautiful bird in the world, is called "doctor bird" because the species' two black streamers remind people of the tailcoat of an old-time physician. Mrs. Havelock has named both birds who return regularly to her feeders.

Into this idyllic garden scene of tea, sandwiches, flowers, petit-point stitching and hummingbirds step three men who represent a ruthless Cuban who demands that they sell their family plantation. When they refuse to sell, the men gun them down in cold blood, assuming that they can pressure the only remaining heir, their daughter, to sell. A peaceful oasis becomes a scene of bloody violence.

M calls 007 to his office a month later and addresses him as James instead of 007, which usually implies that the issue is personal rather than professional. They begin with a philosophical discussion about the lonely nature of the supreme command. An admiral has to decide the orders while others carry out the orders. M, who makes the decisions that affect men's lives, is feeling the burden of his position. M ruminates about the fact that many people become religious in an attempt to pass their tough decisions on to God— but, M reasons, God passes the buck back. God demands that we be tough and make our own decisions. He describes the problem this way: After 40, most people have been knocked about by life's troubles and tragedies making them soft, even dangerous, rather than tough when tough decisions are required.

M gets angry because he doesn't want to make the decision to send Bond on a personal mission. M was the best man at the Havelocks' wedding in 1925. He knows who the killers are, and he knows where they are hiding, beyond the reach of M's department and perhaps beyond the reach of the law. M wants revenge and justice, but he is morally troubled about how to justify taking an eye for an eye. He leaves the decision whether to act to Bond, who weighs the dilemma before him. Bond knows that M is troubled because the victims had been personal friends, defenseless elderly people, murdered by the law of the jungle and beyond the arm of justice.

Like his literary predecessor, Dumas' Count of Monte Cristo, Bond makes the decision to serve as the instrument of divine or community justice. M, in a rare moment of moral cowardice, passes off his personal responsibility and Bond takes on the role of his personal avenger.

The remainder of the tale is the execution of this act. Bond encounters the Havelocks' daughter on her own mission of revenge and justice. She, with bow and arrow, and Bond, with rifle, avenge her parents' murder by killing the three minions and their boss, Hammerstein.

3. From Russia With Love

In the brutal tale of cruelty and romance, *From Russia with Love,* the issue of devotion to duty versus moral cowardice is as significant as the themes of cruelty and malice. Kronsteen, the master chess player who designs a lethal plot to humiliate Bond, M and the British Secret Service, masterfully uses the temptations of lust and covetousness. Kronsteen assumes that he can tempt his prey like this—and he is right. Bond fails to remain vigilant and

You cannot play with the animal in you without becoming wholly animal, play with falsehood without forfeiting your right to truth, play with cruelty without losing your sensitivity of mind. He who wants to keep his garden tidy doesn't reserve a plot for weeds.

—*Markings*, Dag Hammarskjöld

veers from his primary mission. His pride, curiosity and four days of lust-filled lovemaking entice him into the spider's web so carefully crafted by Kronsteen and executed by Tatiana. Meanwhile, M's greed for a decoder is equal to Bond's pride, vanity and lust. The failure to stay on mission nearly costs Bond his life and nearly devastates M and the Secret Service. Before the novel ends, Tatiana Romanova also betrays her mission for love and lust.

Consider these words from the *Letter of James (1:14-16 KJV):*

> But every man is tempted, when he is drawn away of his own lust, and enticed.

> Then when lust hath conceived, it bringeth forth sin: and sin, when it is finished, bringeth forth death.

> Do not err, my beloved brethren.

This passage from the namesake of our hero strikes at the heart of the larger spiritual myth in which the endless, tireless efforts of a tempter are constantly plotting our death and ignominy. This myth unfolds throughout scriptures from the Hebrew texts to the New Testament. Consider this excerpt from the ancient story of Joseph and his master's wife:

And Joseph was a goodly person, and well favoured. And it came to pass ... that his master's wife cast her eyes upon Joseph; and she said, Lie with me.

But he refused, and said unto his master's wife, Behold, my master ... hath committed all that he hath to my hand; There is none greater in this house than I; neither hath he kept back any thing from me but thee, because thou art his wife: how then can I do this great wickedness, and sin against God?

And it came to pass, as she spoke to Joseph day by day, that he hearkened not unto her, to lie by her, or to be with her. And it came to pass about this time, that Joseph went into the house to do his business; and there was none of the men of the house there within. And she caught him by his garment, saying, Lie with me: and he left his garment in her hand, and fled, and got out. And it came to pass, when she saw that he had left his garment in her hand, and fled, that she called unto the men of her house, and spoke unto them, saying, See, the Hebrew mocks us; he came in unto me to lie with me, and I cried with a loud voice: And it came to pass, when he heard that I lifted up my voice and cried, that he left his garment with me, and fled.

—Genesis 39: 6-15 KJV

Or, you'll certainly recall how the temptation to betrayal often calls us at precisely the moment when we should witness, instead, to our most basic values and loyalties.

Now Peter sat outside the palace: and a damsel came unto him, saying, Thou also was with Jesus of Galilee.

But he denied this, saying, I know not what thou sayest.

And when he was gone out into the porch, another maid saw him, and said unto them that were there, This fellow was also with Jesus of Nazareth.

And again he denied with an oath saying, I do not know the man.

And after a while came unto him others who stood by, and said to Peter, Surely thou also art one of them; for thy speech betrays thee.

Then he began to curse and to swear, saying, I know not the man.

And immediately the cock crew. And Peter remembered the word of Jesus unto him, Before the cock crow, thou shalt deny me thrice. And he went out, and wept bitterly.

—The Gospel According to Matthew 26:69-75 KJV

Here is a crucial twist in the Bond saga: In *From Russia With Love,* Bond is most vulnerable to the attack of the agents of *l'empire du mal* because he is suffering accidie. This profound form of listless boredom becomes a perfect portal for the gods who wish to destroy us.

The moral chemistry here is easier to understand than it is to resist. War is filled with passion. Passion focuses the sense of mission. When one is passionless and bored and without the sharp focus of mission, one suffers boredom, even the spiritual flatness and emptiness of accidie. But, lust is passion. It spices up life and renews a sense of passionate focus. So do a host of other lethal temptations.

Falling into accidie between periods of passionate commitment to life's main mission, then, becomes a life-and-death form of impotence. The normally protective barriers we build around our hearts and minds begin to unlock. Accidie lowers our resistance and invites an array of moral choices in the midst of our spiritual weakness. In this sense, all the Bond tales involve accidie and forms of moral cowardice in our weakest moments. Ian Fleming, battle-scarred at the point he wove this fictional cycle, was well aware that evil characters are lurking in such moments—always offering to spice up life with enticing doses of avarice, cruelty, malice, snobbery, self-righteousness and hypocrisy. As a writer, he populated his 14 books with a rogue's gallery of such lethally alluring villains.

Moral Inventory:

First, read the *Letter of James 1:12-16* formatively. Engage your heart. Then, use Howard Thurman's three lines as windows through which to examine your own journey:

"What are you going to do?"

Moral cowardice is the soul of the evil dragon. Moral cowardice occurs when we choose personal gain for pleasure or power, or a God-given mission, above the well-being of the whole.

When have you made a key life decision based on personal pleasure, power or gain? Have you benefited from that decision? In what ways? What did the decision cost you?

When have you made a key life decision based on values and priorities that *superseded* your personal pleasure, power or gain? Have you benefited from that decision? In what ways? What did the decision cost you?

"Who are you going to travel with?"

Recall a time that you've had a sense of calling or vocation about something in your life. How did you sort out that calling—and your commitments to people in you life?

Would you do that differently now? How has your approach changed?

"Don't get them out of order!"

Think of a time when you failed to pay attention either to your work or to the people in your life. What happened when these commitments became unfocused? How did you feel? What did you do? What was the cost?

CHAPTER 002
TWINS OF DUPLICITY 1: HYPOCRISY

But the wisdom that is from above is first pure, then peaceable, gentle, and easy to be entreated, full of mercy and good fruits, without partiality, and without hypocrisy. And the fruit of righteousness is sown in peace by those who make peace.
—James 3:17-18 KJV

As members of religious communities, let's face it: We're hypocrites. If we can't admit that, then we're probably suffering from another malady—spiritual blindness. As respectable and upright as we appear, especially when wearing the yoke of respected professions, we know that we have dark and dirty places within ourselves that we don't want others to see. So, we become good actors to cover ourselves with respectability.

We become hypocrites.

Jesus seemed eager to wrestle with our problem. Hypocrisy drew more words from Jesus than any other subject except the possession of material goods. He identified it as the besetting sin of the overly religious.

> But woe to you, scribes and Pharisees, hypocrites! For you shut up the kingdom of heaven against men; for you neither go in yourselves, nor do you allow those who

are entering to go in. Woe to you, scribes and Pharisees, hypocrites! For you devour widows' houses, and for pretense make long prayers. Therefore you will receive greater condemnation.

Woe to you, scribes and Pharisees, hypocrites! For you are like whitewashed tombs, which indeed appear beautiful outwardly, but inside are full of dead men's bones and all uncleanness. Even so you also outwardly appear righteous, but inside you are full of hypocrisy and lawlessness.

—Matthew 23:13-15, 27-28 KJV

But, of course, hypocrisy is not limited to the overly religious. Hypocrisy is basic to the human condition. We're aware of it and we're just itching to scratch beneath the beautiful facades as revealed daily in tabloid accounts of the famous and powerful. The term "paparazzi" only originated in 1960 and, now, herds of paparazzi all around the world follow in microscopic detail the lives of celebrities and political leaders. This style of coverage has become the hottest genre in American journalism. We eagerly follow such stories because we know that we just might catch a glimpse of our own hidden lives. We all maintain the veneer of respectability, but none of us can be perfectly congruent in thought and action, so we are by definition hypocrites. Like diamonds, hypocrisy is forever.

Paul tells us in Romans to "Behave like a Christian..."

Let love be without hypocrisy. Abhor what is evil. Cling to what is good. Be kindly affectionate to one another with brotherly love, in honor giving preference to one another; not lagging in diligence, fervent in spirit, serving the Lord; rejoicing in hope, patient in tribulation, continuing steadfastly in prayer; distributing to the needs of the saints, given to hospitality.

—Romans 12:9-13 KJV

Ian Fleming's Parable About Hypocrisy: Diamonds Are Forever

A large *pandenus* scorpion emerges from under a rock, the moon over Africa glistening off his black six-inch body and the white stinger arching over his back. A foot below him a small beetle trudges toward new pastures. With ruthless speed the scorpion is atop the beetle, his two fighting claws around the small body. The stinger lances the captured beetle, releasing poison from a lethal sac, and the beetle is immediately dead. The scorpion, always mindful of danger, remains motionless for nearly five minutes, identifying its prey and testing the air for hostile vibrations. Once certain that danger is at bay, the scorpion releases the victim from his fighting claws and begins an hour-long feast with his feeder claws on the flesh of the victim.

This is the opening scene in *Diamonds Are Forever*, Fleming's most theatrical novel, designed to portray the sin of hypocrisy. The stage is set in western Africa in a barren, rocky, desert landscape in French Guinea. At its center is a huge thorn bush as large as a house, the only identifiable landmark over a 20-square-mile area.

The scorpion's greed for the beetle has overridden his memory of rough scraping sounds on the Earth that had been made earlier by boots. As he sucks morsels of flesh from the beetle, the scorpion's instinct detects a slight movement in the air above him. Suddenly a sharp piece of rock cuts through the air, wielded by a heavy, blunt, fingernail-bitten hand. The stone descends rapidly and smashes the creature.

The unfeeling man wielding the rock is a dentist by trade, but also a diamond smuggler. For two hours he has been resting against the thorn bush, watching the drama of the scorpion and its prey as he awaits the pilot who will transport his glittering cache of stolen gems toward their ultimate market. Yawning away his desire for sleep, he hears the distinct sounds of an approaching helicopter. The dentist moves into the open to place lights to mark a landing pad.

When the lights are set, the chopper settles to the desert floor, its rotor clouding the air with debris. As the scene clears, the pilot, a former Luftwaffe ace, cuts the engine and steps out, oozing contempt for his underling. In the pilot's eyes, the dentist is stupid and ill bred, a despised Afrikaner groveling beneath him, worth no more than the scorpion was to the Afrikaner. Both men are links in the multi-national chain of thieves that leads from the African diamond mines to the plush offices of a diamond exchange in London and the theatrical facade of the Las Vegas strip where the diamonds will grace hands and bosoms.

That chain starts with the Africans who mine the diamonds and smuggle them to the dentist in their teeth. The brutality of this "survival of the fittest" is barely visible from atop the smugglers' pyramid, where devious masterminds lie behind the hypocritical elegance of sophisticated, presumptive acceptability.

Diamonds, extracted by slave-like labor, are once again in the news because some of this ill-gotten wealth finances Al Qaeda.

A complex drama unfolds. In contrast to *On Her Majesty's Secret Service*, which includes the word "snobbery" nearly fifty times, hypocrisy is revealed indirectly and metaphorically in *Diamonds Are Forever*. In place of hypocrisy, Fleming's tale is based on the Greek root of hypocrisy, *hupokrinein*, a word sometimes translated as "pretending" or "theatrical." The word refers to acting a part in a play and this is appropriate because the structure of *Diamonds Are Forever* is the closest Fleming gets to classic drama. The opening scene in the remote landscape, for example, has the ominous air of the witches' prologue in *Macbeth*.

Published in 1956, *Diamonds Are Forever* describes the passion for perfect diamonds as akin to the passion for ostentatious perfection that drives hypocrisy. Both worlds are ruthless and cold. Hypocrisy pretends through play-like acting that the imperfect is either not there at all, or, at least, beneath the other's gaze obscured by glistening, jewel-bedecked beauty.

Ian Fleming's own passionate interest in life's deeper substance led him toward collecting first editions of books that altered the course of history, and among his prized possessions was a copy of Charles Darwin's *On the Origin of Species*. Published in London in 1859, Darwin's theory of evolution created a cataclysmic revolution in biology with rippling implications in other scientific fields, but, most especially, in philosophy and theology. Darwin's theories include the assumption that all living beings share a common ancestry and, thereby, are historically and organically interconnected. As if that is not enough to shake mankind's narcissistic perspective, Darwin adds a second major assumption, the theory of natural selection, commonly called "survival of the fittest." At the heart of this theory is the unsettling reality that the variations that constitute the raw material for selection are completely random. This accidental aspect of evolution has had enormous consequences for people whose theological perspective insists on a divine hand carving out the Creation from the beginning. Fleming's chilling prologue to this novel is a distinct nod toward Darwin.

His opening scene of the beetle and the scorpion sets the stage for Bond to traverse the serpentine route up and down the dangerous global chain of diamond smugglers. In this novel, hypocrisy is revealed both in the criminals and, flagrantly, in James Bond.

> Do not judge, so that you may not be judged. For with the judgment you make you will be judged, and the measure you give will be the measure you get. Why do you see the speck in your neighbor's eye, but do not notice the log in your own eye? Or how can you say to your neighbor, 'Let me take the speck out of your eye,' while the log is in your own eye? You hypocrite! First take the log out of your own eye, and then you will see clearly to take the speck out of your neighbor's eye.
>
> —The Gospel According to Matthew 7:1-5

In preparation for his undercover entry into the world of diamond smuggling, Bond joins a policeman in a visit to Rufus B. Saye, suspected of illicit diamond trafficking, the man at the helm of the supposedly legitimate "House of Diamonds." Rufus B. Saye appears to be an honest man who lunches at lovely clubs and lives as a respectable citizen in a comfortable suburb where he plays golf at a stylish club. He doesn't even smoke or drink. The book doesn't mention it, but presumably he's also a pillar of his local temple, mosque or church.

In this early section of the book, Bond also is given a briefing by his chief of staff concerning organized crime in the U.S. However, 007 is so cocky from his recent encounters with extremely evil people that he looks with self-righteous contempt on these American gangsters. His mind mingles stereotypes of Americans with those of Italian gangsters whom he regards as cologne-wearing, spaghetti-eating thugs. There is nothing exceptional about them, in his view.

Irritated with Bond's contempt, the chief of staff informs 007 that those gangsters he is envisioning are merely a front protecting more powerful figures. Rising up the chain, the chief of staff explains, Bond will find ever more powerful criminals. The chief then describes the well-orchestrated network of American crime laced with narcotics, gambling, horses and prostitution. He impresses on Bond that gambling is the biggest industry in America, an industry bigger than steel or motorcars. Bond, nonetheless, remains cocky about his foes.

How quickly Bond has forgotten that he is not playing a child's game. Many of the most ruthless criminals sit hypocritically in the comfort of boardrooms behind soft lights and thus appear removed from the dirty fray of life. However, Bond suffers from the same contemptuous hypocrisy as his newly found enemies, Jack and Seraffimo Spang. Bond enjoys his own luxuries, playing his own privileged role with expensively tailored clothes and bottles of Black Velvet, failing even to acknowledge his own hypocrisy. He hasn't heeded the ancient prophet Amos who admonished those "who drink wine from bowls, and anoint themselves with the finest oils, but are not grieved over the ruin of Joseph!" *(Amos 6: 6)*

Bond is in for a nasty jolt.

Fleming brilliantly portrays the Spangs' hypocrisy. The first element is their pretense of respectability. Living under the alias Rufus B. Saye, Jack Spang pretends to lead a respectable life as the elegant owner and manager of the House of Diamonds. He is a model citizen, so elevated in respectability that he only appears in two scenes of this entire drama. He is literally and figuratively above the dirt of life. However, he is named, along with his brother, in the Kefauver Report as the suspected heads of a syndicate running an illegal wire service for wagering on horses, a gambling casino, narcotics and prostitution networks as well as diamond smuggling. Jack Spang is tucked away so comfortably from these gritty endeavors that he has no criminal record at all.

Bond's route up the diamond-smuggling chain leads him from London, through New York City, to two theatrical menageries: one in Saratoga Springs, New York, and the other in Las Vegas, Nevada. In Saratoga Springs, Bond enters the glittering world of high-stakes horse racing and finds, as well, the lethal world of race fixing. The jockey "Tingaling" Bell, riding Shy Smile, deliberately fouls the favorite, Pray Action, to throw the race and save his own corrupt neck.

Fleming's claim that "gambling is the biggest single industry in America" was based on the Kefauver Report on Gambling from the early 1950s. More recent studies show that legalized gambling alone is a vast, multi-billion-dollar industry in the U.S. and that 15 to 20 million Americans display signs of gambling addiction and nearly 2 million adults are pathological gamblers.

Bond, a veteran of combat with ogres and demons, continues to ooze contempt and disrespect for his current adversaries. Compared to the dragons he has been facing, these thugs seem like B-movie extras.

Before the next act of this play in Las Vegas, the scene in Saratoga Springs shifts to a hellish setting where 007 descends for a mud and sulfur bath in a ramshackle establishment that feels like a Nazi crematorium. "Tingaling" Bell is also at the bath and Bond witnesses the calculated brutality of the gangsters' revenge upon Bell for throwing the race. Now that he has witnessed how far the mob will go to cover their illegitimate operations, 007 begins to take this mob more seriously.

Finally, he heads to Las Vegas. He is moving up the food chain of diamond smugglers and, at the same time, landing in a city that is a crowning expression of theatrical pretense. The Tiara Casino is the global headquarters of Seraffimo Spang and his Spangled Mob. Fleming describes Bond sitting in the casino, observing everything with his professional disdain. Fleming, the keen-eyed journalist and social critic, paints a scene that rivals rings in Dante's *Inferno*. As he describes it, the functional design of the casino attracts and holds its prey much like luring mice into a trap. Here there are wheels and tables and mechanical slots where mostly older women sit, pulling cranks like mice hoping that golden morsels will fall into their waiting cups.

Bond finally meets the most prominent member of the gangland aristocracy, Seraffimo Spang, a playboy with a funny, symbolic name and theatrical hobbies. He's crazy about the Old West and has bought an entire ghost town outside Las Vegas. If we haven't yet figured out that Fleming is pointing us toward higher levels of reflection, he dubs this town not merely a ghost town, but Spectreville. Spang has restored Spectreville with wooden sidewalks, a fancy saloon, clapboard hotel and even an old railway station. Spang is into old trains in a big way. He drives his locomotive, Highland Lights, during riotous weekend parties he caters for his friends. Naturally, Bond is invited to Spectreville and engages in a bar room brawl that surpasses anything in Hollywood B Westerns. The brawl even ends with Spang shouting, "Cut!" At that moment, Bond is once again face to face with an enemy who mirrors the most extreme version of Bond's own evil: theatrical hypocrisy. There stands Seraffimo Spang, dressed in full Western costume, black boots with silver spurs, leather chaps emblazoned with silver and long-barreled pistols with ivory butts draped in holsters on each thigh.

Like a high priest dressed for a ritual, however, Spang has underlings who accomplish the janitorial tasks around his personal altar. Wint and Kidd, from Detroit, are his dispassionate acolytes. It's a moment of wicked, Dickensian satire. Also at Spang's side is another of Bond's damaged women. This sexually abused beauty bears the name most appropriate for this tale of diamonds and hypocrisy, Tiffany Case. When Bond hears her story of degradation he declares to himself that he will never use her abused heart. His compassionate perspective stands in stark contrast to Spang's.

Action swirls on multiple levels. On one level, Spang finally is tearing away Bond's veneer, revealing him to be an agent and ordering his death. Yet, everything else in the story turns to ever more elaborate artifice. Spang doesn't just execute Bond. He orders his pair of mercenaries to perform a Brooklyn Stomping in which Wint and Kidd don football boots and proceed to kick Bond to the point that his will power is shattered and he simply wants to die. This loss of will power, coupled with a death wish, is accidie at its nadir.

The Seraphim are an order of celestial beings or angels who, along with Cherubim and Ophanim, were thought of as guarding the throne of God. In Isaiah's early vision (chapter 6), six-winged Seraphim stood above the throne. The exact origin of Seraphim is uncertain but they were possibly derived from the serpent-like creatures of Assyrian mythology, symbolic of lightning.

What saves Bond in his crushed state is a nocturnal visit by Tiffany, who urges him to fight. Her pull and his own rage revive him. How interesting and appropriate that his genuine struggle for life is engaged only after the hypocritical veneer has been stripped away to reveal his true identity.

Once more it's a case of survival of the fittest as Bond spreads gasoline and ignites the ghost town. As it goes up in flames, James and Tiffany escape the scene on a sputtering railway handcar. Before long, though, they realize that Spang is in hot pursuit in his wood-fired steam engine, The Cannonball. Tiffany and James come to a standstill as their small handcar runs out of gas. The monster bears down upon them. Similar to the role played by Gala Brand in *Moonraker,* it is Tiffany who masterminds the destruction of Spang and his monster Cannonball, cleverly switching tracks and sending the juggernaut careening into a mountain, exploding as if into the fires of Hell.

Bond's up-close encounter with American gangsters results in a new respect for their organization and their camouflage. An intimate encounter is anticipated between James and Tiffany as they clandestinely board the Queen Elizabeth to sail to England and yet Fleming, once again, adds a twist. Bond wrestles with whether he is willing to face the consequences of intimately connecting with this wounded woman. Once again, Fleming poses the issue of private life versus career as a moral decision. The mission is always first. The job is always with him.

And so it is with the mob, as well. The never-sleeping eye of the mob has detected that Bond and Tiffany are heading to sea on the Queen Elizabeth. Wint and Kidd board the ship as well, entering the vessel most respectably, even carrying briefcases! (Oddly enough, Wint's case sports a tag that identifies him as Blood Type F. Never heard of it? Well, it turns out, Blood Type F refers to bovine blood. In truth, he is a bull.)

Fleming continues to toy with layers. Even aboard the luxurious ocean liner with its crystal chandeliers and sauce béarnaise, he exposes the underbelly of life. Among the passengers there will be thefts, fights, seductions, drunkenness, births, deaths, suicides and on occasion, even murder. There's the mutual seduction of James and Tiffany, her kidnapping by Wint and Kidd, Bond's rescue of her and his killing of the thugs.

Hypocrisy is the head of the evil dragon that detests its own tail. Wishing not to claim its full mortality, it theatrically wears a mask of pretense: respectability, even perfection. In theatrical glory, it pretends to be God. This is all toward one purpose: to deny our imperfect, very human lives.

Our drama ends with Bond moving full circle to the origin of the diamond smuggling chain. Back in Africa at the site of the large thorn bush, the dentist stomps a train of ants underfoot while he awaits the helicopter to make his last exchange before he exits the smuggling business. The dentist crushes the black ants and fails to acknowledge the symbolism—his own loathing of all black things. In place of the Luftwaffe pilot is Jack Spang, alias Rufus B. Saye, the remaining leader of the Spangled Mob. He has been traversing the contours of his evil empire, eliminating all the key figures in his dying system. The dentist, confronted by Spang, is like the scorpion he had crushed a month earlier. He senses the raised stone above his own head. The dentist who detested all the life beneath his ruthless hands is killed by the man from the top of his own food chain.

Bond, as the instrument of Divine Justice, has the last word in this contest of the fittest. Working with local police, he fires a rocket at the helicopter rising to take Jack Spang and the most recently smuggled diamonds away from this barren desert. The helicopter bursts into flame and Jack Spang dies. He burns in the crash but it is not the end of the diamonds. Why? Because, even caught in the midst of a fiery crash, they remain indestructible and as permanent as death itself.

Death and diamonds are forever! So is hypocrisy!

Moral Inventory:

First, reread the scriptures: *James 3:17-18*; *Matthew 23:13-15, 27-18*; *Romans 12:9-13*; *Matthew 7:1-5*. Try to read these passages formatively—that is, with your heart—not exegetically—that is, with your mind.

Consider the pressures we all face each week. For clergy, there's the demand of producing a sermon that speaks to scholars in the congregation as well as sixth graders. That pace all but requires references to other published material and sometimes the time and pressure is so overwhelming, clergy borrow whole sermons and pass them off as our own creation. The truth is—similar things happen in nearly every work situation, don't they?

Think of a time when you wanted to keep something hidden— perhaps something you appropriated as your own, as I've just described. Answer the following questions:

What is the "promise" in hiding the truth in such a situation? What is the cost?

What is the "promise" in revealing the truth? What is the cost?

What has been at stake for you in these situations, over the years?

How do you try to resolve such situations? How do you feel about it?

Where did your decisions leave you?

CHAPTER 003
TWINS OF DUPLICITY 2: SELF-RIGHTEOUSNESS

Who is wise and endued with knowledge among you? Show it by good conduct drawn from the meekness of wisdom. But if you have bitter envying and strife in your hearts, do not glory and do not lie against the truth. This wisdom descends not from above, but is earthly, sensual, devilish. For where envying and strife is, there is confusion and every evil work.
  —James 3:13-16 KJV

Of the world's great religions, two traditionally preach that they possess the one true revelation from God: Islam and Christianity. When this particular tenet of the faith is paramount, there is not much room for tolerance. Armed with this conviction, the faithful are certain about the behavior of those within their tradition and equally certain about the heresy of the infidels who are not part of their fold. The righteous are armed with the knowledge that God has shown them the right way, and all other ways are false. Often, the Devil then seems to appear in the other camp or, if a clash arises within our own religious community, it may appear that the Devil has snuck under our tent flap in the form of an unrighteous one who must be purged from our midst.

Understanding the true danger of self-righteousness is crucial, because we tend to regard this problem as a rather benign blemish on the backside of the overly religious. From Dickens and Twain to Hollywood, self-righteousness is standard fare in American comedy. We tend to chuckle about it and forget it, but the truth is: Self-righteousness is a potentially deadly evil, the malevolent force behind war as well as more common forms of pain that we visit on each other for a whole array of religious violations.

In recent decades, many Catholic bishops have helped to streamline their billion-member church's processing of marriage annulments to offer at least a partial step toward healing the church's exclusion of countless divorced and remarried men and women from Mass. While not a form of physical violence, such exclusion has resulted in great pain and separation within families. The noted American Cardinal Edmund Szoka, the man responsible for finally balancing the Vatican's budget in the 1990s, was also a major force behind speeding up the annulment process. Szoka was driven by his own acknowledgment of the pain he had seen among Catholics who were self-righteously excluded from parishes.

In extreme forms, self-righteous enforcement of religious turf can turn lethal. The *Mutaween*, or morals police, in some authoritarian Muslim countries have enforced religious rules with beatings, imprisonment and even death. While this particular form of self-righteous violence is practiced under a veneer of legality in some countries, this proffered claim really represents a continuum that can lead in its most cancerous forms to the lawlessness of terrorism.

The blood of the innocent flowed in more than one corner of the world on August 19, 2003. In Iraq, a truck loaded with explosives reached the corner of the United Nations Headquarters in Baghdad. The crime claimed the lives of Iraqis and foreigners, including one of the most talented United Nations diplomats of his generation, Sergio Vieira de Mello. On the same day a bus bomb in Jerusalem killed at least 18 people and injured scores more, including many children on their way home from the Western Wall. Both despicable acts were committed by self-righteous terrorists whose goal was to disrupt peace, plant fear, take vengeance and thwart the hopes of the majorities of Palestinians, Israelis and Iraqis who do not share the terrorist vision of the world. Imagining their vision superior to that of the majority, and buoyed by their vision of a vengeful god, they deny and disrupt attempts at building peaceful communities.

This has erupted close to home. In 1994, Paul Hill fired a 12-gauge, pump-action shotgun into a pickup truck outside the Ladies Clinic in Pensacola, Florida, killing physician John Britton and his security escort James Barrett, plus wounding Barrett's wife. A Presbyterian minister, Hill called the killings "justifiable homicide" to protect unborn children. He remained defiant until his execution in September, 2003, self-righteously saying he felt no remorse for the slayings and was certain of his reward in heaven.

Terrorism is spiritually rooted in self-righteousness. Behind the eyes of the terrorist is a vision of the world that tolerates no other vision—to the point that all other perceptions of the world must be obliterated at any cost. Terrorists think in absolutes. They are purists.

Here's a simple test for signs of self-righteousness in a person you're encountering: Does this person want to talk *with* me or only *at* me?

When individuals or groups fix the boundaries of a religious tenet, especially one that excludes people, the seeds of self-righteousness are sown. As we close the doors of dialogue, we are declaring: "We know precisely who God is and what Good is, and therefore, we know who the Devil is and what Evil is." We claim to vanquish doubt without realizing that doubt is an essential ingredient of faith. If you doubt this, simply read the journals of countless saints right down to modern heroes like Dorothy Day and Mother Teresa.

And yet there are many examples of religious groups formally declaring that there is no room for doubt or diversity of religious views. On July 8, 2002, the Lutheran Church Missouri Synod suspended the Rev. David Benke, president of the New York-based Atlantic District of the Synod, for participating in an interfaith service at Yankee Stadium for the families of those killed in the September 11th attacks. Benke was suspended for participating with people of other faiths in that service.

Of course, most of us don't need to search headlines to locate the pain of self-righteousness. Over the years, I have heard so many true stories of wounds inflicted in the name of self-righteousness that

I have developed an intolerance of my own: I am self-righteously intolerant of intolerance.

Here's an example of a personal story I encountered:

> She was a small, delicate woman with a quiet voice and a passionate heart of steel. Having grown up with an alcoholic father, she had endured the uncertainty of not knowing what is normal. She compensated with very clear romanticized visions of how her family should look and behave. Her house was spotless. Meals were at fixed times for her two children and husband. Life seemed good and she was thankful each week as she worshipped. Then all hell broke loose. Her husband traveled on his job and became briefly involved emotionally and sexually with an associate. She followed some clues and exposed his adultery, to which he confessed. He wept in remorse and begged for forgiveness, but she was so deeply wounded, fearful, disoriented and angry that she could not risk loving him with forgiveness. She immersed herself in her religion, fueling her bitterness with isolation and the conviction that she deserved to be avenged. Unable to acknowledge her own sinfulness, she became more and more convicted of her righteousness and her right to revenge. In spite of all her husband's and children's appeals, she isolated herself with her own god. She lost her family, but she was right unto the end.

Ian Fleming's Parable of Self-Righteousness: Moonraker

Moonraker focuses on the green baize coverings of club-land bridge tables and the rolling green countryside of Kent. This tale, set in England during one workweek, features Saint George challenging the dragon of self-righteousness. And what a week it is!

James Bond has just returned from the assignment and recovery leave recorded in *Live and Let Die*. M calls James to his office. It is so rare for M to use 007's Christian name that Bond suspects he has been summoned on a personal matter, not a professional assignment.

During the meeting, M questions James about his perception of the prominent multi-millionaire, Sir Hugo Drax. In glowing terms, James describes Drax as a superman who is idolized by many because of his offer to build a rocket that will guarantee England's defense.

Very little is known about Drax's origin. He was found, severely wounded, on the Ardennes battlefield in the winter of 1944 and was identified as Hugo Drax, an orphan from Liverpool. With a gregarious, bombastic personality, he quickly climbed the social ladder. He cornered various commodity markets, especially the market on columbite, a substance with a very high melting point used in jet engines. Drax controlled the supply and named his price until he was wealthy enough to personally finance a super atomic rocket for Britain's defense, dubbed Moonraker. In a letter to the Queen, he gave his entire holding of the columbite ore to the country, plus 10 million pounds. What a man! What a generous benefactor! (Or, as Bond soon will discover: What a self-righteous hypocrite!)

As Bond finishes waxing eloquent over Drax's history, he is shocked to learn that M has received a call for help from the chairman of Blades, a gentlemen's gambling club mentioned in several Bond tales. In this hallowed hall, no one has charged Drax with cheating yet, but he's winning too regularly and too often. The stakes are high and the threat of scandal is disturbing. In this society, where appearance tops substance, cheating at cards is about the only sin that can destroy a man, we are told. However, Drax is so accomplished at cheating that no one has caught him yet. Time to bring in Bond … James Bond.

Bond agrees to observe Drax at Blades and, if necessary, take him on and teach him a lesson. This is possible, because Bond has been sent by his Ministry for training as a gambler and qualifies as a card shark himself, a master of duplicitous maneuvers. (After all, the term "duplicity" comes from gambling and refers to double-dealing.) Dressed in a white silk shirt, Navy serge suit, dark blue socks and well-polished black moccasin-style shoes, Bond drives toward Blades thinking of the drama about to unfold with Drax.

Fleming adds graphic touches to his mythic drama as Bond spots a bewildering sign in the sky that seems to proclaim: *HELL IS HERE*. However, when he stops his car and positions himself at a better vantage point, the sign's full text is revealed: *SUMMER SHELL IS HERE*. Of course, as readers, we've already received the nudge from Fleming and the stage is set for Bond to confront the Dragon in Hell.

> *Doubtless the pleasure is as great of being cheated as to cheat.*
>
> —*Samuel Butler*

The gauntlet of Blades forms the gates into this Hell. The club, we are told, opened in the last quarter of the 18th century as a male oasis of dining, drinking and gambling. Known as the Ace of Clubs, it is the essence of elegance and duplicity, a seat of the aristocracy. But Bond quickly discovers that Drax is at odds with Blades' culture. It turns out he is bombastic, arrogant and sweats profusely. He is as ugly in flesh as he is in spirit. Fleming likes to paint his demons as severely ugly and Drax ranks among the ugliest. In German, *Drache* means "Dragon," and this Anglicized embodiment, who calls himself Drax, certainly has a horribly reptilian appearance. And there's more! Fleming tells us that this Dragon sports one of the classic traits of the Devil: red hair.

The image recalls Dante's description of Geryon, the monster in the *Inferno* who represents Fraud:

> It had the features of a righteous man,
> benevolent in countenance,
> but all the rest of it was serpent.
> It had forepaws, hairy to the armpits,
> and back and chest and both its flanks
> were painted and inscribed with rings and curlicues.
> So many vivid colors Turk or Tartar never wove
> in warp and woof or in embroidery on top,
> nor were such colors patterned on Arachne's loom."
>
> —Dante Alighieri, *The Comedy: Inferno*, XVII, 10-18

There also is a surprising message in the title of this Bond tale that underlines all this imagery. For years, I assumed that *Moonraker* referred to how high Drax's rocket soared—so high that it raked the moon. Only recently did I learn that Moonraker is a nickname used in Wiltshire where Fleming owned a home. Wiltshire was the home of many smugglers famous for hiding their booty at the bottom of ponds to deceive the authorities. This worked well until the moon shone brightly, revealing the booty to any investigator looking into the clearly lit water. As the story goes, any sighting of inspectors would prompt the smugglers to begin raking the surface of the water, causing bubbles and disguising the booty. As they performed this odd activity, they would claim to be making cheese on the surface of the water, which seemed like an empty-headed folk tale to the police, concealing not only the loot but also the genius of these masters of fraud.

Upon arriving at Blades, Bond makes himself a sweet bundle: 15,000 pounds, to be exact. He achieves this feat by stacking decks and using other deceptive strategies to defeat Drax overwhelmingly at bridge. Not much money to a multi-millionaire, but a sizable sum to the civil servant.

The evening perplexes Bond. Why would a wealthy man, idolized by so many, stoop to cheating at cards? This behavior may seem as strange to us as reports of movie stars shoplifting. Fleming argues that the problem lies in the core of the self-righteous heart. Such a person perceives himself as above the common will and behavior of people. Public opinion and communal preference don't matter because the self-righteous live in a capsule of superiority and scorn. Their position places them so far above the muck of ordinary human life that the self-righteous begin to assume it is their right to win, their right to all the rewards around them. Since they should never lose to lesser beings, cheating is an acceptable tool. To the self-righteous, the ends justify the means in witch-hunts and in cards.

Hypocrisy is the natural cover for such an arrogant soul, a lethal combination. Hypocritical self-righteousness is about perceived height. Those who envision themselves towering above the common herd of mankind are responsible only to the vision behind their own eyeballs. The bitter irony is that these twin towers of duplicity—

hypocrisy and self-righteousness—place the evil person above and beyond the possibility of reconciliation, redemption and community.

He also told this parable to some who trusted in themselves that they were righteous and regarded others with contempt.

Two men went up to the temple to pray, one a Pharisee and the other a tax collector. The Pharisee, standing by himself, was praying thus, "God, I thank you that I am not like other people: thieves, rogues, adulterers, or even like this tax collector. I fast twice a week; I give a tenth of all my income." But the tax collector, standing far off, would not even look up to heaven, but was beating his breast and saying, "God, be merciful to me, a sinner!" I tell you, this man went down to his home justified rather than the other; for all who exalt themselves will be humbled, but all who humble themselves will be exalted.

—*The Gospel According to Luke, 18: 9-14*

After his defeat of Drax, Bond is called back to M's office. This time he is going on duty in the field. Never have his assignments been within England, but this time he is being sent through Kent to the Dover cliffs, the site of Drax's Moonraker launch. All the personnel at Drax's compound are Germans except for two, a security officer and Drax's personal secretary, Gala Brand. Gala is an undercover agent who has been on the job since its inception. James Bond and the lovely, brilliant Brand are sent off by Drax to explore the beach under the white towering cliffs.

Still under the delusion that the Moonraker is a legitimate gift to England, they set about looking for possible routes where saboteurs might invade the site. That is, until a dynamite explosion above sends tons of white rock raining down upon them. They survive, barely and bare.

James and Gala now know that they are targets, but they lack sufficient information to blow the whistle. Ironically, they're used to acting alone even against the odds of conventional assumptions, which in itself is a self-righteous modus operandi. Brand has been keeping careful calculations of the gyro settings for the guidance of the Moonraker. Often miffed that Drax seemed to disregard her calculations, always recording his own projected settings as well, she suddenly discovers what has been unfolding. Drax intends to send his atomic missile soaring toward the heart of London. The whole plot turns out to be the years-long culmination of Drax's self-righteous thirst for revenge against the British.

Tricked by Drax and captured, Bond and Brand are taken to the rocket silo where they are threatened with torture. Bond reveals that both of them work for Scotland Yard and their capture is unknown by the authorities. In typical Fleming style, we again see Bond, captured by his evil enemy, hearing the dragon's confession.

Drax's real name is Graf Hugo von der Drache. His mother was English, so he was reared and educated in a country he resented, but he completed his education in Berlin and Leipzig. In World War II, Drax became one of the German commandos, known as Hitlerjugend Werewolves, who infiltrated behind Allied lines as saboteurs at the time of the Ardennes offensive. Dressed as an English soldier behind Allied lines, Drache was nearly killed in an explosion. When he recovered, he was thought to be an English soldier. He played the part and was sent from hospital to hospital for recuperation. During that year he formulated his plan for revenge.

Bond and Brand are left bound in the rocket silo to fry to a crisp but manage to free themselves just before the rocket leaps into the sky toward its target. Just as Tiffany Case saves Bond's world in *Diamonds*, it is Brand who devises the plan to save England. Bond had planned to go under the rocket and strike his cigarette lighter, igniting the escaped fuel, thus sacrificing himself to save the millions in London. Gala, who had kept track of the gyro guidance numbers, has Bond climb instead into the rocket to redirect the Moonraker to its intended test course into the North Sea.

Immediately before the rocket is launched, Drax delivers a radio message to the entire nation. He also leaves a lengthy letter with solicitors in Scotland to be opened and published following the launch of Moonraker. Drax's snarling messages of self-righteous revenge are worth reading as you reflect on Fleming's layered themes in this novel.

Finally, back in M's office, Bond muses about whether the pigeon who lands on the windowsill might be the same one who had landed there five days earlier. How close this pigeon came to vanishing. The heart of a nation might have been silenced—millions blotted out by the will of a self-righteous sociopath, but for an amazing sequence of events that included a controversy over cards, a brilliant woman's head for physics and the courage of a loner agent. There seems to be a larger pattern here that works toward good, rather than evil, Bond speculates. He wonders: Whose pattern?

Self-Righteousness is the loftiest head of the evil dragon. From a position of imagined superior height this swelled head lives, isolated with his or her own almighty, vengeful god, casting scorn and contempt on all the lesser beings for whom there is only negative judgment, and with whom there is no community.

Damn! Just as Bond is about to give us his philosophical/theological answer, M's squeaky old chair swivels round. We are left to answer this important question: Is there a larger design, a pattern, to this confluence of events?

For their courage, loyalty and superior execution of duty, both Bond and Brand are offered the George Cross award. She accepts, but Bond's department prevents any public notoriety for his work, so he is denied the esteemed award. He can't collect the other possible reward, either, for Gala is engaged to be married. So, once again, Bond doesn't get the girl. He has suffered two quick losses after saving his country. He remembers the thoughts he had upon defeating Drax at the gambling table, that a winner's gain always feels less than the loss to a loser—failure often feeling so much larger than the delight born of success.

Denied both honor and love, Bond remains a secret silhouette—although this final twist may be the chastening discipline that saves him from the chief temptation in *Moonraker*, self-righteousness.

Moral Inventory:

First, read the *Letter of James 3:13-16* formatively. Engage your heart.

Then, ponder and even journal about your own self-righteousness. Remember, if you decide to write, feel free to keep your notations private. You may want to use the following lines as starting points for your reflection:

Self-righteousness often stems from wounds, real or perceived. Is this true for you?

Is your self-righteousness honed to a sharp edge on the grinding stone of revenge?

Sometimes an individual must take a stand against the crowd. How do we discern the difference between motives of true justice and temptations toward self-righteousness? Some religious traditions, including the Quakers, organize discernment groups to help face this common challenge. What steps have you taken to help sort out such issues?

Sometimes an individual has the opportunity to bridge the chasm between two warring, self-righteous factions or persons. If you've had that opportunity, you might want to discuss what happened in a group. If you haven't faced such a challenge, then how would you go about such a task?

CHAPTER 004
TWINS OF VIOLENCE: CRUELTY & MALICE

From whence come wars and fighting among you? Do they not come from lusts that war within you? You lust, yet have not. You kill, and desire to have, and cannot obtain; you fight and war, yet you have nothing, because you do not ask God. You ask, and receive not, because your asking is amiss, desiring only to consume what you may receive within your lusts.
    —James 4:1-3, KJV

O LORD, how long shall I cry, and thou wilt not hear! I even cry out unto thee of violence, and thou wilt not save!
Why do you show me iniquity, and cause me to behold grievance? For spoiling and violence are before me; strife and contention rise up before me.
Therefore the law is slack, and judgment never goes forth: for the wicked compass about the righteous; therefore wrong judgment proceeds.
    —Habakkuk 1:2-4 KJV

"With malice toward none..."
    —Abraham Lincoln, March 4, 1865

often cry over our daily news. Like the Prophet Habakkuk in the Hebrew Scriptures, I am filled with grief at the daily broadcast of violence. So often, the victims are the innocent and vulnerable among us. Despite this steady diet of woe, here are three vignettes of cruelty and malice that stunned me.

True Story No. 1: An elderly man, who had suffered a stroke but had recovered, was driving along a road slightly below the posted speed. Like many stroke survivors, he simply moved at a slower pace. But, it was not fast enough for the driver behind him who, after flashing lights, rammed his vehicle into the rear of the slower driver's car. The ramming proceeded until the car in front stalled. By now, the impatient driver was fully consumed by addictive rage. He pulled the older man from his car and pummeled him to death.

True Story No. 2: A Border Patrol agent picked her up at 5:15 a.m. as she staggered slowly along an unlit, deserted street. He thought she must be drunk, but when he viewed her in the light, he saw bruises and scrapes on her face and arms along with a blackened eye. She said she was walking to a funeral. Her oldest brother had been murdered. When she told her husband that she planned to attend the funeral, he laughed and beat her. When he fell asleep, she snuck out of the house and began the long walk to the family funeral.

True Story No. 3: The couple who sat with me for counseling was not atypical, although he was so convinced of his own brilliance as well as his own special brand of misery, that he thought his life and suffering unique. This gave the rationale necessary to justify his nightly drinking. He is a prominent businessman, and she manages their household and cares for their children. They profess to be devout believers and active members of their church. What brought them to me was his personal lack of zest for life, his sense that family and finances had burdened him unfairly, and finally his feeling that his wife did not appreciate him. She was quiet and reluctant to talk about life in the home because of fear. But the truth was soon on the table that physical violence occasionally accompanied his drinking. The steadiest diet of abuse was verbal and emotional. We weren't together long until he said to her, in my presence, that he surely would be a happier man if he weren't married to such a stupid and crazy woman. When I challenged these demeaning remarks, he was nonplused. He was convinced of his accuracy. She turned out to be the brighter, cleverer, healthier person, who had lived too long in an abusive arrangement.

We all need to talk more about the violence that is so integral to our lives. This is difficult, so I will start with myself, admitting that I have a cruel side that surprises and disturbs me when it occasionally emerges. What's the situation in my home? Well, I have always thought of myself as gentle, kind and compassionate. Through the years, that is the feedback I have received from others and kindness is my dominant posture, but not my constant one. There have been stresses and strains within our home, some of which I've mentioned in the course of this book. Judith, my wife of 45 years, has suffered from chronic, debilitating migraines for the last four years. For the first eighteen months of this four-year stretch, she suffered incapacitating pain, day and night. Our lives altered radically. Many of our retirement dreams have been shelved, and our roles have been more defined. On the whole, I have been a compassionate, gentle caretaker. On occasion, though, I have been cruel with words and less than comforting with my actions.

We all need to shine more light on this common temptation toward violence, because it so easily breeds fear, chaos, confusion and terror in our souls. But let us look closely at the ambiguous nature of violence. There are forms of violence that are sanctioned by society, even revered as sacred. The American Revolution and countless other revolutions were born of violence that was sanctioned, even enshrined after the fact. The U. S. Civil War is still called by some southerners the *Second Revolution*. Who writes the history and on which side of the rampart one stands determine whether the violence of the moment is just or unjust, whether the actors are terrorists or freedom fighters. For example, in various eras and in various segments of American life, the abolitionist John Brown was denounced as a terrorist— and honored as a saint.

All warriors enter battle with a mythology that makes their killing enemy soldiers acceptable. I have a very dear friend who was a warrior, a man dedicated to his profession, undergirded by his warrior mythology. I asked him to write a brief statement about his personal journey because I believe he models the spiritual journey many of us need to make. He writes:

> When I was nine, my father was killed on the battlefront in Korea. At that young age, I committed myself to follow in my father's path. I graduated from West Point and spent twenty-six years in service to my country including two thirteen-month tours in Vietnam. As a soldier's soldier, I lived accepting the Greek and Roman mentality: "Come home victorious carrying your shield or come home dead and laying on it." I accepted the reality that I lived on the moral edge and that I had probably killed at least seventy-five enemy soldiers. I also had held many nineteen-year-old comrades in my arms as they died.
>
> During the last days of US involvement in Vietnam I had long conversations with fellow soldiers who were being sent on missions to enter bedrooms to kill Vietnamese civilians whom the U.S. command couldn't take out of the country or leave there. There was no place in my warrior mythology for this killing. It violated a deep sense of duty and ethic at the heart of my being. I returned home as a resigned, dejected and confused man. I diligently sought a new mythology to frame my existence. I hired a guide to journey with me. I meticulously wrote a journal as I read Dante's *Inferno*, searching my own soul for a way through Hell, to a redemptive path and a new mythology to frame my future.

This man's courageous journey is a model for our time. This kind of pilgrimage through Hell toward a new mythology of life—a new understanding of our sacred purpose in life—is unfolding all around the world. It's the path C.S. Lewis and J.R.R. Tolkien followed out of the trenches of World War I. Today, it's the challenge facing former "child soldiers" if they try to return to their villages in Africa. As Lewis, Tolkien, Vonnegut, Fleming and my friend who served in Vietnam all discovered, this search for a new mythology is our one hope for reframing the sacred boundaries of life in light of our own violence.

For a time, my friend's *warrior mythology* was the container in which he could place the violence of war. The greater challenge today is grappling with the meaning of violence when no container seems possible due to the utterly random, recreational or abusive nature of the violence. Who could hope to contain, for example, the horrific violence child soldiers are forced to inflict on others in some global conflicts? Yet, the challenge remains at the core of our human condition and the very core of this book.

Violence lies even at the heart of the Christian story. The Crucifixion is an act of violence repudiated by the Resurrection. The victim becomes the arbiter of peace, compassion and forgiveness. A violent tearing lies at the heart of that story and appears to run through all creation, past and present. Even the birth of a child is a violent tearing with the anticipation of the cry of new life's joy.

Ian Fleming's Parables About Cruelty & Malice

The James Bond tales are peppered with violence, sadism, cruelty and malice. James Bond is sometimes described as a man with a cruel mouth whose demeanor is ruthless and cold. Fleming was not promoting violence. He wrote parables to expose the evils of cruelty and malice and, in them, Bond often used violent methods in his quest to save the world or at least the fair maidens in distress.

Personal stories from Fleming's life add irony to the focus on the twins of violence: cruelty and malice. John Fishman, author of several best sellers, was Fleming's colleague for nearly twenty years. Fishman was the senior editorial executive in the same newspaper organization in which Fleming was foreign manager. Fishman records that Fleming liked to say that people only have the right to kill what they will eat— and nothing more. *(For Bond Lovers Only,* compiled and edited by Seldon Lane, Dell Publishing, 1965; Jack Fishman presents 007 AND ME by Ian Fleming, p. 22)

Certainly, this seems an unlikely statement from the creator of fiction laced with so much violence, but it underscores my basic point that the Bond tales were not intended to encourage cruelty and malice, but to expose their dangers through parables. A nearly identical statement by Fleming appears in the opening of *The*

Hildebrand Rarity, when Bond is pursuing an extraordinarily evil-looking stingray with the intent to kill it. We are told that this was unusual for Bond because he rarely killed fish, except for food.

There also is an oft-repeated story concerning Prime Minister Anthony and Clarissa Eden's visit to Goldeneye, Fleming's house in Oracadessa, Jamaica. During the Suez crisis in 1956, Eden's health deteriorated under the extreme political pressure, so he and his wife borrowed Goldeneye as a tropical retreat. They spent three weeks there in late November and early December, 1956, and the Prime Minister returned to England on December 14, suntanned and relaxed. His health broke again three weeks later and he resigned his Premiership. The Edens only had one complaint concerning Goldeneye: rats. The rats squeaked and broke things in the night, awakening the Edens. Once the servants supposedly said, when Sir Anthony organized a rat hunt: "Commander Fleming does not like them to be killed. He says they cannot help being bush rats."

Fleming's aversion to killing seems to have been personal. In early 1941, Fleming was secretary to the Director of Naval Intelligence, Admiral Godfrey. In that role, Fleming traveled to the United States with his boss on an extremely important confidential mission. The men were to meet with J. Edgar Hoover and other key persons in an attempt to coordinate intelligence operations between the two nations. Hoover appeared initially to brush-off these two Englishmen. It turned out that Hoover already had specific channels of communication with Canadian millionaire Sir William Stephenson, whose organization represented British Intelligence in the United States. Sir William Stephenson, often called the Quiet Canadian, welcomed Godfrey and Fleming and paved the way for their delicate mission. Stephenson's British Security Co-ordination was well established in an office on the thirty-sixth floor of Rockefeller Center and had already rendered invaluable service to British Naval Intelligence. Stephenson, a World War I fighter pilot, an amateur boxing champion, was also a millionaire by age thirty from his invention of the radio photograph transmitter. Ian Fleming, an incurable hero-worshiper, idolized Stephenson.

While in New York, Fleming and Godfrey were exposed to the subversive operations of Stephenson's company. Fleming personally accompanied Stephenson and his agents on a night-time raid of the office of a Japanese cipher expert who was transmitting delicate information to Tokyo. At three in the morning, Stephenson, his two agents and Fleming entered the Japanese agent's office, cracked his safe and borrowed and microfilmed the code books before returning them exactly to their previous place. This great piece of espionage was later embellished in *Casino Royale* as Bond reports shooting a Japanese cipher expert in Rockefeller Center. (It was one of two missions that earned Bond his oo classification. Actually, Fleming borrowed the oo designation from the official Naval Intelligence classification for top-secret documents.)

The focus of Fleming's June, 1941, visit to the U.S. was to establish co-ordination of intelligence work. There was no coordinating office in the United States in these months prior to Pearl Harbor; in fact, there was no secret service in the U.S. at that time. There was rivalry among the various departments. They had no Homeland Security coordinator to reduce competition between the Navy, Army, State Department and FBI. The Quiet Canadian was making inroads with Roosevelt toward establishing the office of Coordinator of Information and securing his candidate, General "Wild Bill" Donovan, Roosevelt's former legal aide, as the appointed official in charge of all forms of intelligence and covert operations. When this appointment was made on June 18, 1941, Fleming disappeared for two days. When Fleming finally left Washington he took with him a .38 Police Positive Colt revolver, a personal gift from "Wild Bill" Donovan. The inscription on the revolver reads, "For Special Services." The special services were, as verified by Fleming's life-long personal friend, Ivar Bryce, that Fleming was sequestered under armed guard for two days to write, based on his own knowledge of British Naval Intelligence, a seventy-page description of the administrative structure and operational format for the American Coordinator of Information. (*You Only Live Once*, Ivar Bryce, p. 54) This model later became the format for the creation of the OSS (Office of Strategic Services) later to evolve into the Central Intelligence Agency. Ian Lancaster Fleming was rewarded "For Special Services" toward the future establishment of the CIA.

On a later visit, Fleming joined his friend and hero, Sir William Stephenson, at his secret training camp for covert operations at a farm complex on the shores of Lake Ontario, near the village of Oshawa. Allied agents were being trained there and Sir William thought Fleming would gain by the experience. So Fleming was trained by experienced underwater and hand-to-hand combat experts. He learned about the tactics and techniques for espionage, the intricacies of ciphers and code-breaking, silent breaking and entry, radio transmission and detection. Fleming participated in many exercises and excelled at underwater drills and with the machine gun. He learned judo. On a special assignment to plant a bomb in a Toronto power plant, Fleming called the plant director and introduced himself as a British engineer. He easily penetrated the station grounds and clandestinely planted the fake bomb.

Stephenson, interviewed years later, said that Fleming was an exceptional, courageous trainee but had too much imagination to be an agent. Sir William told the story of Fleming's final exercise. One of the instructors was from the Shanghai Police, trained and extremely skilled at dodging bullets. This man went to a cheap hotel in Toronto. Fleming was given his address, room number, a loaded .38 revolver, and was instructed to track him down and kill him. The test was to determine if he had the nerve and ruthless resolve necessary to kill another man. Stephenson made sure Fleming's gun was loaded and told him this was serious, no more games. Sir William and other agents were watching from secret places as Fleming got to the landing of the hotel. There he stood for a long time. He turned and left. Later Fleming apologized to Sir William, explaining that he could not kill a man that way.

What was the lingering impact of these amazing true-life experiences? Fleming's friend John Fishman, in the 1960s, reported that Fleming talked about violence in these terms:

> Like all fictional heroes, Bond has to reflect his own time, and we are in what is perhaps the most violent era man has known. Thirty million were killed in the last war, some six million of them simply slaughtered, mostly brutally. I have been accused of inventing fiendish cruelties and tortures for my stories, but the torture scenes in my books are no worse—if as bad—as what happened to Allied agents during the last war. No one who knows the things

that were done to captured agents or what went on in
Algeria would level this criticism at me.

Clearly, Fleming was a man uniquely poised at the heart of the 20th Century, one foot firmly based in older mythologies of violence—and the other one mindfully stepping toward what might be a new mythology. *From Russia With Love* is precisely such a tale.

From Russia With Love

Violence, cruelty and malice coupled with romantic fantasies, seductions, and sex are the threads that form *From Russia with Love*. Grounded in Cold War mythology, this tale moves upward into the cosmic struggle between good and evil, the forces of light against the forces of darkness.

Bond does not appear in the first third of this tale. Instead, we are introduced to the merciless, meticulous, malicious people plotting Bond's death and ignominy. Why kill a man unless you can ruin his reputation also? The executioners of the plan are cold, indifferent, calculating agents of violence. They are instruments of the Devil from *l'empire du mal*. Their plots are hatched near Hell's furnace.

Among the foes in this novel is Red Granitsky, code name "Granit," a deserter from the British army who has become the Chief Executioner of SMERSH, the artful killing machine of the Soviet Special Services. Once again, he's a character who repulses people, but there is an intriguing twist here. This time, the bad guy is not physically ugly, yet his masseuse loathes him and cringes at touching his body. Part of this is physical: his cruel, thin lips, his asexuality, his totally indifferent demeanor. But, his masseuse makes it clear to us that his cruelty is deeper than physical appearance. It's a spiritual matter, a beautiful body containing an evil soul.

As Fleming unfolds the opening scenes of this epic, the directors of SMERSH gather as moguls of death, crafting a plan for their next victim. As underlings of the Devil, they are bound in common fear of each other. The High Praesidium demands an act of terrorism in the intelligence field that will not disappoint the Devil and will shame the enemy. Unlike SPECTRE, which is Fleming's fictional creation, SMERSH was an arm of the KGB, as were some of the key names and places chosen for this tale.

The architecture of this mythology is startling. These moguls of death must peer through Hell's furnace door into the heat that radiates from the enormous power of the High Praesidium and craft, then execute a plan that will bring both death and shame to the enemy. This is quite a challenge. How can they shame the British Secret Service? Is there a hero they can target? Colonel Nikitin finally breaks the silence. Hesitantly he names such a hero: Bond … James Bond.

In charge of this meeting is General Grubozaboyschikov, a real Russian whom Fleming names in the novel. As the general signs Bond's death warrant, we learn that it specifies Bond's death must be with *IGNOMINY*.

The strategy falls to Colonel Klebb, head of the department of SMERSH in charge of Operations and Executions, once again a physically repulsive foe. Klebb is a wicked, toad-like woman with a ruthless will to survive even as she destroys the lives of her victims. She summons to her team Kronsteen, the Russian national chess champion, whom she engages each time she plots a murder. Kronsteen, a man without moral values, is not interested in human beings, even his own children. He plays chess with people's lives and even ranks their most potent temptations: self-preservation, sex, and the instincts of the herd.

As a Fleming villain, Klebb is best remembered for her style of interrogation, a symphony of sadism she conducts seated on a campstool, poised so close to the face of her victims that she can inhale their screams as a kind of delicious perfume. As conductor, she merely whispers numbers to accomplices, coaxing them to apply specific tortures, yet she remains almost aloof. She hovers over her victim, cooing like a dove, calling out endearments like a loving mother—pulling secrets from them with this merciless abuse. This is malice in a form so potent that we almost want to turn away in disgust.

But this stratagem for killing with ignominy requires an even more devious form of manipulation, calling on the dedicated service of an extraordinarily gorgeous woman. The beautiful Tatiana Romanova is set up to seduce Bond without compunction by her bosses, since they regard her gorgeous body as virtually inhuman, a possession of the State.

If this mythology sounds familiar, you're probably recalling President Ronald Reagan's famous rhetorical confrontation with the "Evil Empire." Reagan may have gotten this phrase from Anthony R. Dolan, his fiercely conservative speechwriter, or from Alexander Solzhenitsyn's 1975 AFL-CIO speech, or from the chief of French Intelligence Alexandre de Maranches, who flew to Los Angeles in 1980 to warn Reagan against *l'empire du mal*. Reagan's *Evil Empire* sermon, delivered on March 8, 1983, to the National Association of Evangelicals, brought praise from conservatives, disdain from liberals, outspoken criticism from foreign governments, but it was historian Edmund Morris who pointed out that American media largely missed the reaction of ordinary people within the Soviet Union.

For years, Solzhenitsyn and many other Russian writers, including the poet Joseph Brodsky, had seen the basic contest playing out on this level. It's what shaped the slogans that spread across eastern Europe in 1989, such as Vaclav Havel's famous banners in Prague that proclaimed: "Truth and love will conquer lies and hate." Morris points out that Reagan's prominent use of the phrase "Evil Empire" was an important early signal to many within the Soviet empire that the United States finally was engaged in the ultimate conflict.

This isn't a history lesson. It's as relevant as tomorrow's headlines about global foes like Osama bin Laden. We misunderstand Al Qaeda's allure if we regard it merely as a political party with a violently assertive platform. Bin Laden and his followers have even stepped outside the classical boundaries and traditions of Islam to form their own new global mythology. Thomas Friedman makes this argument, as well. We are not engaged in a clash of civilizations, Friedman argues, but a struggle against super-empowered individuals like bin Laden who are weaving their own new mythologies about our world.

So, how does our hero, Bond, rise to Fleming's new challenge? At the outset, he is compromised. He has lost his edge. He is a man of war, and the peace is killing him. We finally greet Bond as he awakens bored and sluggish in the midst of bureaucratic malaise. He has let down his guard; his sense of mission is mired in the routines, papers and daily grind of life. He is bored, afflicted with accidie, the only vice Bond utterly condemns. If the gods wish to destroy us, we are told, they first will make us bored.

Fleming, who took great pride in his own Scottish heritage, probably was drawn to stories that some of Lermontov's ancestors came from Scotland. Russian Information Agency press releases in the 1980s, during Lermontov's 175th birthday, affirmed a Scottish link to the Russian writer's family, although other sources dispute a Scottish tie to Lermontov. Even more intriguing is that Lermontov's own literary hero, Pechorin, was an infamous lothario engaged in international intrigue, who suffered devastating depression and loss of all will to live after a romantic encounter with one particularly beautiful woman. Perhaps Bond should have done a little more literary homework before leaving home.

This global chess match, designed by Kronsteen, opens as Tatiana Romanova contacts a British agent in Turkey, Darko Kerim, with the offer to defect with a cipher decoder. She will defect, machine in hand, if the man she loves will meet her and escort her to England. M's greed for the machine makes him eager to take the risk. Bond's lust for a mysterious new lover seduces him into Homeric blindness. He sets sail already wounded by Kronsteen's masterful strategy.

Of course, Bond wants to know how this siren even knew to call out his name.

M briefs him. We learn that Tatiana told Darko Kerim that she worked in the Central Index of the Soviet Secret Services for six years. One of the files she constantly handled concerned Bond. She had his picture and knew extensive details about him and fell in love with him so completely that she hopes to defect and join the man she loves. She even points out that her favorite book is by the 19th Century Russian writer Mikhail Lermontov about a hero who spends his life getting in and out of difficult adventures.

This fanciful parable of cruelty and malice takes Bond on an odyssey that reaches from the sewers of Istanbul to a gypsy camp where two lust-filled women fight to the death to win their man. Bond participates in the cold-blooded murder of an enemy. Then we travel the Orient Express with its aura of mystery, lust and violence, and finally we wind up in a Paris hotel where Rosa Klebb, with poison-tipped darning needles and venom-tipped, switch-blade shoes, finally brings Bond down. We do not learn until the next tale, *Doctor No*, that the poison hospitalizes Bond for six weeks. He is expected to die and his survival is labeled nothing short of a "miracle."

Violence is the sharp tail of the evil dragon. It slashes willingly, coldly, indifferently, with sadistic, ferocious cruelty and malice toward all who will not bow down before it. It thrives on the power attained in the moment. It connects perpetrator and victim, breeding separation and isolation.

If we haven't glimpsed the larger adventure yet, then *From Russia with Love* makes it clear that we are visitors in the creative workshop of a writer pulling together resources from around the world to hammer out his new mythology.

Moral Inventory:

Read the *Letter of James 4:1-3* and *Habukkuk 1:2-4*. Engage your heart. Then, ponder or journal about your own experience with cruelty or malice—not only incidents in which you have been a victim, but also your own temptation toward these twins.

Consider these questions:

Violence is all around us. At the heart of many sports is violent competition. Many of us have come to accept competitive violence as part of our entertainment. Movie special-effect designers now compete to depict ever more grisly scenes. At what cost do we accept this violence in our daily lives—and for what promise do we accept this?

Violence is often integral to personal and social change around the world. Again, weigh the cost and the promise of choosing violence.

Violence is at the core of the basic stories of our great religions. Review some of the texts from our tradition, if you are not familiar with the level of violence described and even approved in many cases. In Bible study, read passages from Joshua, for example. Weigh the cost of this violence in our traditions and the promise involved in such stories.

Don't leave this reflection on an abstract level. Think of a time when you were violent, specifically cruel or malicious in your actions. Then, answer these additional questions:

What was at stake for you in this situation?

What did you do?

How did you feel?

Where did this leave you?

Violence often stems from our own wounds, real or perceived. Was this true for you?

Sometimes an individual has the opportunity to bridge the chasm between two warring factions or persons. If that opportunity came to you, how would you approach this task? Would you employ violence as part of your approach?

CHAPTER 005
TWINS OF POWER 1: AVARICE

Now, ye rich, weep and howl for your miseries that shall come upon you. Your riches are corrupted, and your garments are moth-eaten. Your gold and silver are cankered; and the rust of them shall be a witness against you, and shall eat your flesh as it were fire. Ye have heaped treasure together for the last days. Behold, the laborers who have reaped your fields, whom you have defrauded, cry out to you; and their cries have entered into the ears of the Lord of sabaoth. Ye have lived in pleasure on the earth, and been wanton; ye have nourished your hearts, as in a day of slaughter. Ye have condemned and killed the just; and he doth not resist you.

—James 5:1-6

Because thou sayest, I am rich, and increased with goods, and have need of nothing; and know not that thou art wretched, and miserable, and poor, and blind, and naked: I counsel thee to buy of me gold tried in the fire, that thou may be rich; and white raiment, that thou may be clothed, and that the shame of thy nakedness not appear; and anoint thine eyes with eyesalve, that thou may see.

—Revelation 3:17-18

Jesus said to them, "Take heed, and beware of covetousness: for a man's life consists not in the abundance of the things which he possesses."
And he spoke a parable to them, "The ground of a certain rich man brought forth plentifully: And he thought to himself, saying, What shall I do, because I have no room to bestow my fruits? And he said, This will I do: I will pull down my barns, and build greater; and there will I bestow all my fruits and my goods. And I will say to my soul, Soul, thou hast goods laid up for many years; take ease, eat, drink, and be merry. But God said unto him, Thou fool, this night thy soul shall be required of thee: then whose shall those things be, which thou hast provided?" So is he who lays up treasure for himself, and is not rich toward God.
—Luke 12:15-21

Once upon a time there was a very selfish and wicked peasant woman. When she died it was said that there was not one good deed of hers that could be remembered by any of her neighbors. So awful was she that the devils immediately claimed her as one of their own, grabbed her and threw her into a lake of fire. Her guardian angel struggled, though, to remember one good deed from the life of the woman to present on her behalf to God. Finally, the angel went before the throne of God and said that one time the woman had pulled an onion out of her garden and gave it to a beggar woman. God's response was that the onion would be her key to Paradise. The guardian angel was to take the onion stalk to the old woman and offer to pull her out of the lake of fire. If she was pulled from the lake by the onion she would go on to Paradise, but if the onion broke she would remain in the lake of fire. The angel offered the onion to the old woman saying that it was her means to salvation. She grabbed on and was easily pulled from the fiery water. But, other sinners saw her being pulled from the lake. They grabbed her by the ankles hoping to be dragged along. The old woman began kicking and screamed at the sinners saying, "I'm to be pulled out, not you. It is my onion, not yours." With those words, the onion broke and the old woman slid back into the lake of fire. The angel slowly left the shore, weeping.

This classic tale from Dostoevsky illustrates how avarice can become as much a part of life as breathing. Of course, we see such greed reflected in daily headlines, sometimes involving corrupt CEOs who seem to care little for employees, stockholders or customers. Studies show that Americans' assumptions about the corporate world have shifted in recent decades. Younger adults entering the work force have little expectation that employers will care for their future, assuming that they will have multiple employers throughout their lives and that they will have to protect themselves and their future.

How much has avarice entered our hearts? In our commodity-driven culture, we seem to need more and more things with each passing year. In fact, studies of consumerism have shown that Americans today list far more *necessities* in life than Americans did a decade ago. For example, now personal computers, cell phones, microwaves and air conditioning are considered necessities by huge portions of our population.

I have acknowledged owning each of the deadlier sins. Some have been more convicting than others; none is more disturbing to my soul than avarice. This shocked me because I have not viewed myself as an avaricious man, nor do I live ostentatiously, but when I read the passage in which James Bond refused a million-pound bribe with the simple words, "I have enough," I was palpably soul-jolted. I grew up in a fairly poor family, living with grandparents until I was in the 10th grade because my parents could not afford a house. I began working when I was twelve to contribute to the family coffer. When I read, "I have enough," I realized that I have lived my entire life on a scarcity model, believing I did not have enough. I have lived a lie. I do have enough.

This Bond parable was placed in front of me as a mirror about the same time I first went to Cuba in 1998 to live and work among people whose average salary was $7 to $10 a month. Accepting the reality that I have enough was reinforced by living among people who celebrate life in spite of their meager holdings.

Part of our nation's legacy was a moral structure that restricted luxury and self-indulgence and emphasized temperance, hard work and frugality. This moral dream was shattered in the 1960s and '70s with our loss of the war in Vietnam, the assassinations of JFK, Robert Kennedy and Martin Luther King. Countless other events, including the Watergate scandal, conspired to shake our dream of who we are as a people. We were in a spiritual crisis and, like a glutton who turns to the refrigerator to fruitlessly feed a deep hunger in the soul, we turned to money and consumption as a balm for our aching, disoriented souls. Marketing experts molded our wants into needs; bankers offered easily obtained credit cards and risky mortgages; states opened lottery sink-holes and so on. This fundamental shift in our culture has led us to the edge of financial and spiritual chaos.

Ian Fleming's Parable About Avarice

Ian Fleming said he loved writing larger-than-life myths, and *Goldfinger* is Fleming in his grandest mythic style, weaving a tale about avarice. In this novel, written in 1959, Bond faces Auric Goldfinger, an incredibly wealthy tycoon who nevertheless cheats at cards and golf. If there's any doubt about the mythic nature of the tale, consider the parallels with the ancient King Midas of Phrygia. Among other things, Goldfinger is as physically grotesque as Midas, whom Apollo angrily disfigures with donkey ears. Here's a summary of the ancient myth:

> Greeks and Romans elaborated on the story of a real king, named in the archives of the Assyrian Empire as "Mita of Mushki." The wealth of Phrygia reached its height under Midas and may well have inspired the tragicomic tales about this greedy man's comeuppance.
>
> In one version, the king meets the oldest and wisest of all satyrs, Silenos, a companion of Dionysus. The satyrs or nature spirits were known for their wisdom and love of wine. Midas spikes the fountain in his rose garden with wine and captures Silenos when he comes for a drink. Eager to understand the meaning of life, Midas imbibes wine with Silenos and seeks the wisdom of the satyr.
>
> Ovid adds a twist to the story: Dionysus, grateful for the satyr's safe return, grants Midas's wish that all that he touches will turn to gold. Midas dashes about exulting in his golden touch, transforming twigs, stones, apples, clods

of dirt into gold. Hallelujah! But when it is time for dinner he watches aghast as his bread turns into golden lumps on his golden plate. As his lips touch the wine, it flows as molten gold from a golden goblet. Unlike the modern Goldfinger, Midas doesn't need to paint fair maidens with gold. When Midas touches his own daughter, she instantly turns to solid gold.

Midas begs the gods' forgiveness. He is cured by a plunge into the River Pactolus, whose stream has ever since carried gold sand. But alas, there is more to the tale.

One day Midas passes by when Pan and Apollo are conducting a musical contest. Apollo strums his lyre and Pan plays his pipe. All agree that Apollo's lyre is sweeter, except Midas who favors Pan's pipe. Apollo is enraged and executes swift punishment by replacing the king's ears with those of a donkey. Eager to hide his embarrassment, Midas begins wearing a purple turban. Only his barber knows the truth, but he can't contain his secret. He whispers the secret to the earth, which tells the reeds, who reveal Midas's shameful secret each time they rustle in the breeze.

In Fleming's tale of Bond and a modern Midas, we also encounter contests—a crucial card game and a lengthy golf match. Fleming, through Bond's reflections, also reminds us of divine intervention in the form of coincidence or Providence. At one point in the dramatic golf match, Bond actually exclaims: "A sign from Heaven!" Before it ends, the novel becomes a confessional for both Bond and his nemesis.

Goldfinger is a classic Fleming villain—a compact package of such potent greed and lust that Bond actually envisions popping a light bulb in his mouth to see all that energy palpably aglow! Like other Fleming demons—Red Grant, Sir Hugo Drax and Scaramanga— Goldfinger has two of the Devil's traditional traits: ugliness and red hair.

Bond's first encounter with Goldfinger seems coincidental. Bond is asked to help a friend who has been losing constantly when playing cards with Goldfinger. Bond is suspicious when the friend tells him about Goldfinger's quirks when playing, including a claim of agoraphobia, a fear of open spaces, that requires Goldfinger to take a specific seat at their canasta games. Bond exposes Goldfinger's cheating and, along the way, there's another nudge by Fleming about the larger associations he wants us to make: Bond unpacks his Walther PPK, which he has packed inside a fake book, titled, *The Bible Designed to be Read as Literature.*

After this coincidental encounter over cards, M and Bond meet to discuss the very villain Bond has just bested. Goldfinger, who presents himself as a respected jeweler, metallurgist and distinguished member of Blades and the Royal St. Marks at Sandwich, now is suspected of conspiracy to finance the murder of hundreds through SMERSH. And so, our dashing hero sets off in further pursuit of Goldfinger, this time armed with golf clubs. If you read this particular Fleming novel, don't overlook the asides Fleming keeps handing us between dramatic sequences. In this instance, you will find Bond pondering the cosmic nature of coincidence itself. He wonders that Providence could have crossed his path with Goldfinger's twice in such close proximity.

Coincidence and Providence are threaded though all the Bond tales, especially the 18-page golf match between Bond and Goldfinger. God becomes almost a third player on the course. The match unfolds at Royal St. Marks where Bond hopes to defeat Goldfinger once more and thus impress this tough-minded competitor enough to win an invitation into Goldfinger's inner circle. In a key putting situation part way through the match, Providence shows up almost on Bond's command. Read the passage as the players approach the tenth hole and you'll find both an invocation and Bond's exclamation of thanks to divine forces.

This is Ian Fleming's universe, though, so Bond isn't headed toward Heaven. Instead, he winds up with his invitation to Goldfinger's gloomy, morgue-like home. There, Bond meets one of the most famous villains in modern literature, the ruthless chauffeur-bodyguard Oddjob.

The next day, Bond tries to sneak back into the compound when he encounters another person lying in the grass. This is Tilly, who explains to him that she has come to kill Goldfinger because he murdered her sister—the same woman who helped Bond in the incident with the cards. Tilly gives us a gruesome description of Goldfinger's fetish: hypnotizing women so that Oddjob can cover their bodies in paint, except for an area on the back that supposedly allows the skin to breathe. Then, Goldfinger possesses his glittering mistresses as if he is marrying the gold. Some women then are paid and sent away, but Tilly's sister was entirely encased in the gold until she died.

Fleming was inquisitive and acquisitive. He carried a notebook in which he frequently jotted scientific, mechanical, logistical and geographical details. He also benefited from researchers' and volunteers' contributions of information. The latter group included a Col. Geoffrey Boothroyd, an expert in firearms whose letters prompted Fleming's switch from a Beretta, which Boothroyd considered a "ladies' gun," to the more powerful Walther.

This revelation stuns Bond. For once, he is overcome by guilt over a death and confesses that his moral priorities are tragically awry. *Goldfinger* contains more than one confessional, though. As often happens in Fleming's novels, Bond winds up in Goldfinger's clutches. He survives near death under the whirring teeth of a giant circular saw, but winds up a pawn in Goldfinger's ultimate avaricious plot, robbing Fort Knox. While still a captive, Bond hears Goldfinger's confession of avarice, an addiction to the color, glow, texture and "divine heaviness" of gold. It's a vivid example of a man consumed by a deadly sin.

In Goldfinger's reverie, he envisions himself in the world's leading ranks of mountain climbers, deep-sea explorers, astronauts and scientists. Like Adolf Hitler envisioning grandiose stone monuments with his architect Albert Speer, Goldfinger boasts that his crime at Fort Knox will be considered a mark of genius around the world for centuries to come. It is the titanic scale of this crime that finally lifts Bond's struggle onto the mythic stage: a St. George locked in a battle to the death with the Devil. In fact, Bond himself tells us that Goldfinger's crime will rival Cain's murder of Abel. Eventually, the two foes are locked literally in hand-to-hand combat, choking each other. Bond's fingers prevail and Goldfinger dies.

> *Avarice:*
> *Avarice is the voracious, unappeasable, and omnivorous head of the evil dragon that wants, gets and keeps more than it needs. Avarice is driven by fear and a lonely, insatiable power-hungry tail.*

It's a potent metaphor for us today, isn't it? Perhaps more than any of the other deadly sins, avarice has us by the throat. In *The Canterbury Tales*, Chaucer describes avarice in this same fashion as if the sin involves clutching things so tightly that we nearly smother ourselves in the process. In his famous 14th-century cycle of tales, he wrote:

> Avarice, after the description of Saint Augustine, is a desire in heart to have earthly things ... And the difference between Avarice and Covetousness is this: Covetousness is for ... such things as thou hast not; and Avarice is to withhold and keep such things as thou hast, without rightful need.

Moral Inventory:

First, read these scriptures formatively: *James 5:1-6, Revelation 3:17-18, Luke 12:13-21.* Think about your own consumption. It may help to journal, writing down a list of everything you own that you would call a *necessity* in your life. Be honest about this. When researchers want to study this issue of *necessities*, they sometimes ask respondents to "list those things that, if they break down, you would immediately replace without a second thought."

If you're careful in this exercise, you'll be surprised at the length of your list! Compare lists with younger or older people and see if you can discern generational differences in need.

How much of this consumption would you call an addiction? How much of it is rooted in avarice? How much of it is simply practical human need?

What do you think is driving our increasing consumption? Better products? Better advertising? Real changes in our lives?

Many states now have lotteries to help fund programs ranging from education to elder care. Do you play the lottery? Why? Stop and think through your motives carefully. Do you think there's a moral choice involved in playing a lottery?

Research the texts of your religious tradition concerning money and material goods. You may be surprised to find that Jesus had more to say about our use of money and material goods than any other subject.

Think of a choice you've had to make between what you own—and the well-being of the whole community. Talk about such situations with friends. How did you make your decision in this case?

CHAPTER 006
TWINS OF POWER 2: SNOBBERY

If there come unto your assembly a man with a gold ring, in goodly apparel, and there come also a poor man in vile raiment; and ye have shown respect to him in gay clothing, and say unto him, Sit here in a good place; and say to the poor, Stand there, or sit here under my footstool: Are ye not then partial in yourselves, and are judges of evil thoughts?
  —James 2:2-4

I n *On Her Majesty's Secret Service,* Fleming calls snobbery "that most insidious of vices." He was speaking from years of painful acquaintance with its sting.

Fleming was born May 28, 1908, to Valentine and Evelyn St. Croix Rose Fleming, as the second son of a wealthy, socially prominent Scottish family. Ian's paternal grandfather was an investment banker and a self-made millionaire. Ian's mother claimed Sir Richard Quain and John of Gaunt among her ancestors. Ian's father had invested a large portion of his inherited wealth in real estate prior to his death on a World War I battlefield on May 20, 1917. His death, a tragedy for the family, was notable enough that the obituary printed in the London Times was written by Winston Churchill, a fellow Conservative M.P. Ian Fleming grew up in the upper stratum of the complex British class structure where status and value were first calculated from lineage.

In 1952, Fleming married Ann Charteris. She recently had divorced her second husband, Esmond, the second Viscount Rothermere. The Fleming marriage was passionate and very rocky. Ann's previous husbands had complained about her social and literary friends and Fleming was no different. She was drawn to her friends near London and he to his writing assignments. Ann and her friends mocked and derided Ian's writing. But the ruthless negative criticism of Fleming was not limited to this personal circle.

The negative critics of Bond and Fleming were, and are, endless. The most famous drubbing of Fleming was Paul Johnson's hatchet job in the *New Statesman*, titled *Sex, Snobbery and Sadism*, in which Johnson described *Dr. No* as "the nastiest book I have ever read," and added:

> There are three basic ingredients in *Dr. No*, all unhealthy, all thoroughly English: the sadism of a schoolboy bully, the mechanical, two-dimensional sex-longings of a frustrated adolescent, and the crude, snob-cravings of a suburban adult. Mr. Fleming has no literary skill.

Fleming certainly stirred the moral pot and also stood socially on a peak from which critics eagerly sought to topple him. He regarded their barbs as intellectual snobbery. Within his own life, Fleming experienced the same moral battlefield as his literary hero, facing many of the same temptations that lured Bond. Once, Fleming boasted that as much as his wife enjoyed high-class parties, he would take "a cheap joint any day." True to his boast, he had a taste for strip-tease clubs and other entertainments traditionally associated with lower classes.

He stood painfully astride these social strata, well aware of the complex nature of this particularly devilish sin of snobbery. At its core, he knew, snobbery is racism, classism and elitism. It does not ask about what you believe, what you have done, or what you will do with your life. In the form of classism that was so prominent in Fleming's world, snobbery asks: Who are your dead? This form of snobbery is a high window on the world viewed through blood and ancestry. All these forms of snobbery tend to hate a faith that believes in forgiveness, redemption from sin and an eternal future unfolding in life with others and with God.

Snobbery may sound like an old-school temptation, perhaps something encountered in BBC television reruns and not worth more than a curious smirk over our shoulders. So, let's bring this issue much closer to home. Right now, for example, many leaders within Christianity and Judaism are charging that traditional condemnation of homosexual men and women is a form of snobbery. However you feel about this issue, you may be surprised by some of the voices raising this very point, including popular evangelical voices like Tony Campolo, Brian McLaren and Rob Bell, all of them best-selling authors of books read especially by younger Americans. Gallup data over the past decade indicates that the desire to condemn gay people by some older Americans is not a cause for concern among younger adults—and, with each passing year, the age of acceptance of this diversity rises. As this book goes to press in the autumn of 2008, new nationwide polls show that a majority of all Americans has at least accepted legally acknowledging civil unions between same-gendered couples. You may be strongly opposed to this new inclusiveness, but millions of Americans who once considered opposition to homosexuality to be a safe, majority attitude are discovering that their traditional viewpoint is beginning to look more and more like snobbery.

In my own personal journey, I have become ever more welcoming of diversity. I was born in a poor, white family in the hills of southwestern Pennsylvania and grew up in Erie, PA. We were Protestants living in a predominantly Roman Catholic, Eastern European community. Following seminary, I was the founding pastor of a rapidly growing interracial church that, after 40 years, has become even more ethnically balanced. As a pastoral counselor, I was profoundly influenced by clergy colleagues from all traditions, sexual orientations and genders. Five years ago on our 40th wedding anniversary, my wife and I wrote a Letter to the Editor to voice our appreciation of diversity. We wrote, in part:

> Today we celebrate our 40th wedding anniversary. For us, marriage is committed friendship through which each

of us has grown in wisdom and virtue because of the friendship. We have been able to serve a greater good for ourselves and our community because of our marriage friendship.

We have gay friends who have lived a long time in a committed friendship rearing two adopted children. Both are deeply spiritual and very committed to their religious faith community. They are not promiscuous and the intimacy of their friendship has enabled each of them to grow in virtue and wisdom for the good of the community. Why can we not see this kind of committed friendship as Christian marriage?

Perhaps this disclosure of my views makes you uncomfortable, because this is still a very close-to-the-heart moral issue for millions on all sides. This book isn't a Bible study on this particular issue. I am raising this intensely emotional issue to demonstrate the still-potent problem of snobbery. Perhaps you don't regard your attitude toward homosexuality as snobbery, but our society seems to be moving toward a more inclusive consensus. Snobbery isn't a quaint issue from the past; it's an intense issue people are wrestling with today.

The Pedigree of Honey
Does not concern the Bee—
A clover, any time, to him,
Is Aristocracy.
   —*Emily Dickinson, c. 1884*

As in all things Christian, let's turn to Jesus as a welcome model of conversion when we face the power of snobbery in our lives. Many Christians insist that Jesus was perfect from infancy through the end of his life, but that assertion is challenged by at least some New Testament texts. If we believe that Jesus was a real human being who grew throughout his life, then we may even be witnessing Jesus rebuffed for snobbery in passages such as *Matthew 15:21-28* or *Mark 7:24-30*. These are scenes in which Jesus encounters a foreigner, a mother whose young daughter has been possessed by "an unclean spirit." When this woman pursues a weary Jesus and pleads with him to heal her daughter, he snaps that it would be like tossing bread to dogs. The woman is persistent, though, and snaps right back at Jesus. Suddenly, Jesus softens, relents and performs the healing.

Some commentators rebel at the idea that Jesus was chastened by this woman and actually changed course because of her rebuke. Perhaps these commentators fear that a woman played such a catalytic role or they fear accepting a Jesus who was not entirely perfect at every moment in his life. For me, this passage only leads me to love Jesus more. It makes his humanity real. He was a man who could acknowledge broader worldviews. Just as so many women have enabled me to broaden my perspective on life, it appears that a persistent and rather desperate woman of a different ethnic heritage was instrumental in converting Jesus from what may have been a weary moment of snobbery.

Ian Fleming's Parable About Snobbery

Fleming, along with the author of the *Letter of James*, considered snobbery one of the most insidious evils. Fleming brilliantly portrays this evil in the mythic parable *On Her Majesty's Secret Service.*

Ernst Stavro Blofeld appears, with altered physical characteristics, in three novels: *Thunderball, On Her Majesty's Secret Service* and *You Only Live Twice.* This kind of shape-shifting is another trait of the Devil; and Blofeld's ability to reincarnate himself so effectively makes him a dragon worthy of our modern St. George. He clearly is a villain close to Fleming's heart. For example, Blofeld was born in Gdynia of a Polish father and a Greek mother on May 28, 1908, the same day as his creator, Ian Fleming. More than any other demon in Bond's life, Blofeld also embodies the evil of accidie that plagued both Bond and Fleming, a temptation we will explore in the final chapter.

Blofeld uses his ill-gotten fortune to finance a vast criminal network called SPECTRE: the Special Executive for Counterintelligence, Terrorism, Revenge and Extortion. In our own era of burgeoning social networks from the benign Facebook to the terrifying Al Qaeda, Blofeld's world is fascinating to examine. He actually infuses his own social network with a kind of ethical value system. When one of his men sexually assaults a captive that SPECTRE is holding for ransom, Blofeld returns part of the ransom and executes his guilty underling. Perhaps it is this quest to establish himself at the pinnacle of a new social order that lures Blofeld toward a fatal dalliance with snobbery—a claim that he is the noble Comte de Bleuville in *On Her Majesty's Secret Service*.

Teresa's story shows us the ingredients in spiritual accidie, the focus of our final chapter. You'll understand more about this deadly sin if you read Teresa's full story in Fleming's novel. She had everything, resulting in a sense of endless power, and then she lost it all. Idealization, the belief that heaven can be made on earth, and unfinished grief combine to form the soil in which spiritual accidie grows.

The entire novel toys with layers of social status and snobbery. While Blofeld is hatching his plot to unleash biological warfare starting with Great Britain, Bond is enjoying himself in France and preparing a letter of resignation from the Secret Service. Ironically, their mutual pursuit of new social connections is what places them on a collision course. In Blofeld's case, it is his pursuit of a noble title while trying to dominate the world. In Bond's case, it is his pursuit of a tragically beautiful woman, La Comtesse Teresa di Vicenzo, eventually leading to their ill-fated marriage.

Bond meets this girl in classic Fleming style—through an impromptu race between their sports cars in France. They wind up in a casino, where he wins big and she loses big. He graciously pays her debt. He claims to resent snobbery and yet reveals himself as a thorough devotee of such luxurious environs. Only later, over drinks, does Bond discover that the beautiful Teresa harbors suicidal feelings, a form of spiritual accidie. She confesses that her life is no longer worth living, making her a perfect match for Messieurs Bond and Fleming. The next day Bond attempts to rescue her as she walks into the sea to kill herself. Instead, both of them are kidnapped and taken in a small skiff to a secret location to meet Marc-Ange Draco.

Here begins one of the most delightfully human exchanges in all of the Bond books. These two professionals represent opposite sides in their global struggle. Nevertheless, Bond, who supposedly is on the side of the angels, listens to a painful story of personal loss from this criminal whose name is angelic. Marc-Ange is a Corsican bandit, head of Union Corse, an organized-crime network throughout France and her colonies. He reveals that the matter of deepest concern to him at the moment is not professional, but personal, concerning his daughter, Teresa.

Snobbery is the jeweled head of the evil dragon, seeking status and power by diminishing the masses and attaching to the few. Snobbery is the worship of the dead. It is an attempt to gain power and status by blood, not by faith or personal deeds. At its core, snobbery is racism, classism and elitism.

Marc-Ange tells the story of his own wild-spirited English wife, who had died ten years earlier, and the birth of his only child, Teresa. While Teresa seemed to have every advantage in life, Marc-Ange explains that some "worm of self-destruction" is eating away "her soul." Her tragic story includes a brief but terrible marriage and the death of her only child from that union. As Marc-Ange concludes his tale, he admits to Bond that this is the first time he has told this story to another man. Bond responds by asking if therapy—or perhaps the consolation of the church—might help.

The result is one of the strangest pacts in Fleming's fiction: Marc-Ange asks Bond to help save his daughter by courting her and eventually marrying her. He promises Bond one million pounds in gold. This is the moment I referred to earlier in this book, when Bond shocks us with his refusal of this fortune, saying that he has enough to meet his needs already. But it is only the money Bond is refusing. He agrees to court Teresa, if she gets therapy and recovers.

He also asks Marc-Ange to help him in his pursuit of Blofeld, which leads Bond to Blofeld's secret mountain lair in Switzerland.

Here's where Fleming delves most deeply into the lure of snobbery. In this novel, pay attention to the scenes involving the College of Arms in London, where Blofeld is pursuing his claim to be the Comte de Bleuville. There are a couple of deliciously Dickensian scenes in which Bond investigates this musty agency, where one employee admits, "Snobbery and vanity positively sprawl through our files." It's in the early pages of this novel that this same functionary telegraphs the tragic outcome of the novel both for Blofeld and for Bond, warning Bond that the pursuit of such snobbery ultimately belittles pursuers until "they dwindle and dwindle in front of you."

Fleming was a passionate collector of books and ideas. The Fleming Collection, now housed in the Lilly Library at the University of Indiana, is full of books that were integral to the development of modern science and culture, including their evil manifestations. Among the volumes are four by a man who has been called Adolf Hitler's French mentor, Joseph-Arthur Comte de Gobineau. In the 1850s, Comte de Gobineau proclaimed that race is unchangeable. He championed the Nordic or, as he called them, Aryan peoples as the elite, destined to rule all of mankind. That Blofeld wants to be validated as Comte de Bleuville may well have its roots in Fleming's knowledge of the racist Comte de Gobineau.

The stakes in this case rise, as M and others in authority over Bond urge him to destroy Blofeld but warn that the Swiss are unlikely to cooperate. So, Bond turns to Mark-Ange for help and asks that Marc-Ange's wedding gift be assistance in destroying Blofeld. Suddenly Bond, the instrument of divine justice, finds himself working with the other side in an attempt to bring about the termination of a greater evil. Their collaboration does not entirely succeed. They destroy Blofeld's arsenal, but Bond winds up severely injured and Blofeld once again escapes. Their greatest success may be the blossoming love between Bond and Teresa, who are united in marriage after Bond sufficiently recovers.

But the fruit of snobbery usually is tragedy for all concerned and there is a final twist in this novel, which I won't reveal here except to say that it represents snobbery's bitterest legacy.

Moral Inventory:

First, read the following passages formatively: *James 2:1-4; Matthew 15:21-28; Mark 7:24-30.*

Then, think about the nature of snobbery. We all are afflicted to some extent. What forms of snobbery do you find in yourself? Do you find yourself trying to conceal such attitudes? Have you ever been caught in an uncomfortable moment in which your own snobbery was challenged?

How important is family lineage in your self-identity?

It may be easier to identify signs of snobbery in your community, your social network, even in your congregation or denomination. What signs do you see? What are the origins of this behavior? What are its promises? What are its costs?

CHAPTER 007

ACCIDIE

God giveth more grace. God resisteth the proud, but giveth grace unto the humble. Submit yourselves therefore to God. Resist the devil, and he will flee from you. Draw near to God, and he will draw near to you. Cleanse your hands, ye sinners; and purify your hearts, ye double minded. Be afflicted, and mourn, and weep: let your laughter be turned to mourning, and your joy to heaviness. Humble yourselves in the sight of the God, and God shall lift you up.
   —James 4:6-10

For godly sorrow worketh repentance that leads to salvation not to be regretted, but the sorrow of the world worketh death.
   —II Corinthians 7:10

Create in me a clean heart, O God;
And renew a right spirit within me.
The sacrifices of God are a broken spirit;
A broken and a contrite heart,
O God, thou wilt not despise.
   —Psalm 51:10, 17

We have new neighbors; the elderly man and woman who lived in the house for more than forty years have moved out. A young family with two children has moved next door and the sounds of children playing once again fill the air. They seem like joyous, innocent children at ages six and eleven. Of course, they yell and scream and tease and occasionally bicker, but it is Matthew, age eleven, who especially delights my soul. Matthew loves to sing. He sings at the top of his voice, often melodically, with great gusto. He sings for long periods of time whether playing alone or with his sister and other children. He sings as a child filled with joy. I love hearing him celebrate the joy of innocence and life.

How long has it been since you sang with great joy? Were you ever filled with a deep and prolonged joy? If you were joyous and are no longer so, what squelched or crushed the joy in your soul? What feeling replaced the passion and vitality of joy? Were you ever able to restore the sense of joy and, if so, how did you accomplish this?

When we lose our passion and joy for life, we may have slipped into the spiritual condition known as accidie. I want to share a couple of stories that capture the essence of accidie. They show the contrast to Matthew's innocent joyous singing:

> He was the clerk making a replacement key for one I had lost. I admired his forthrightness! His honesty was clear, clean. His honesty also conveyed his grief and pain. I commented on a tattoo that showed below his rolled sleeve.

> He said, "I've got them all over me. I'm part Cherokee and I have one on my chest and a huge eagle that covers my back. It was stupid. I did it when my world fell apart. I held a job for 13 years and got laid off. I came home to find my wife in bed—my bed with another man. Things got real crazy. I did some stupid things—these tattoos are some of 'em."

Another clerk came close and he stopped talking, but I knew in an instant that I had heard another man's pain, witnessed his scar.

What happens to us when life doesn't hold sacred what we rest our world upon? When our dreams get dashed on the rocks, how do we cope?

In the spring of 1994, I delivered a sermon titled "Saturday's Child" on accidie at St. Mark's Episcopal Church, Capitol Hill, DC. This vibrant congregation has countless persons who came to DC with the dream of making a difference in our nation. They have given their lives through dedication and hard work and, except for small victories, many live with an ache in their soul, as if their dreams were tacked to a tree. My words on the ancient sin of accidie named and touched something deep in many people that morning. Even before using the word accidie, I described the kind of person likely to fall prey to this temptation:

> It is often the sin of those who are dreamers and romantics and idealists. It is often the sin of those of us who believe hard, and work hard, and live hard; those of us who throw our whole selves into our work, and our marriage, and our church, and our friends, and our country and our children. It is often the sin of those of us who believe that we can make a difference in this world.

I described the sin of accidie using the words of St. John of Damascus:

> … a sorrowfulness so weighing down the mind that there is no good it likes to do. It has attached to it as its inseparable comrade, a distress and a weariness of soul, and a sluggishness in all good works which plunges the whole person into a lazy languor and works in him or her a constant, slow, lazy bitterness.

I also revealed my own source of sorrowfulness and accidie by confessing the impotence I have often felt when attempting to make a difference in people's lives. Here is what I told the congregation that day:

I have felt that whatever I do, it wouldn't make much difference anyway. I'm just like a peanut in Redskin stadium. I know that there are people who are hungry and cold at night. I know that there is intense racial and sexual discrimination in our country. I know that the nuclear issue hangs over our heads. I know that there are countless issues I could put my energy into, but I get the feeling that there is nothing that I, little me, unappreciated me, could do which would make much of a difference anyway. So I pull up closer to my comfortable fire, wrap the comforts of life around me and feel better, yet quietly bitter and despairing about the way this life is.

Now I want to make it very clear that we are not talking about the kind of morbid depression that is the result of physical or mental illness. I am describing a spiritual condition. I am speaking of the moods that come over normally healthy Christian persons, moods that we are tempted to indulge rather than resist. Don't we all know in varying degrees that grey mood that settles on our soul, when nothing seems really worth doing, when meaning drains out of our lives? When we find it hard to respond with real interest to the things we care about, when we tend to despair of ever being better or stronger characters than we are now and we take a soft, cynical view of the people around us and of life in general. In fact, sometimes, we are not sure we believe that life is good at all.

Let me see if I can take you a little deeper into this condition. The Christian faith is captured metaphorically in three days: Friday, Saturday and Sunday. Friday, the day Jesus was tacked to a tree, the day in which his spirit was broken. Saturday, the long day of waiting, some say the day he descended into Hell. Sunday, Easter morning, the day of the resurrection of Jesus, which made him our Christ.

Where are you on your own Christic journey? Are you in Friday, or are you, like most of us, trapped in Saturday, or have you reached the "Yes" of Sunday morning? Look at it with me.

Friday: Now before we can get to Friday, we need to look at our innocence. We need to look deep in our soul for what we yearned for, what we dreamed about, what we believed this world would be like. The deep, deep down vision that you had for what your life would be like and what this world would be like, for your marriage or for your country or for your family or for your children. But every one of us has hit a Friday. Every one of us has been thrown up against the rock, or tacked to a tree, and our dream has been devastated and our innocence has been violated. And that's the Friday of our lives.

When was your spirit broken? What broke it? And did it almost destroy your faith in the goodness of this life or the goodness of God? For some of us, it goes way back. Our very innocence was destroyed very early by an angry mother or a distant or absent father, by alcohol in the family, or by physical or emotional abuse. For some of us, it was the death of the Kennedy brothers. For others it was the death of Martin Luther King. And for some of us it was the death of someone else we idolized. One woman told me recently that when she was seven years old, her uncle, the man she believed in, the man who had shown her the goodness of life, died of cancer. After that, she said "Something in me wasn't sure where God was, and whether I could believe in goodness any longer."

For some of us it was taking our senior trip in Vietnam. And for others, it was when our marital dream died. Or when we dreamed of whom we were supposed to be in this world, but we didn't open that door. Or we didn't have the children that we thought we would have, or we had more children than we thought we would have, or a child of ours became mentally ill—or a child of ours died. On the Fridays of your life, the pain is excruciating, and it is very appropriate to be angry, enraged and in deep grief.

But most of us can't keep living in Friday, and so we move to Saturday. We can't stay in the intense pain of Friday and we haven't yet been able to say the "Yes" of Sunday morning, so we live in Saturday.

Saturday: Many of us are Saturday's child. For Saturday is the janitorial day of life. It's the errand day; it's the get-through-it day. It's the day when the grief and the anger can combine into a flat, soft, lazy, cynical bitterness. It is a kind of spiritual deadness. It is a kind of life in which you don't feel any spice, any real vitality or any vigor—it is spiritual accidie.

At that point, we are ready to commit the following three sins. We either get into having affairs through our lust, or we eat too much through our gluttony, or we try to buy everything in the store through our avarice, to fill the ache in our empty heart. It is the day when we refuse, by our pride, to surrender to the way life has come to us. It is the day we accept our inertia, our cynicism, our bitterness as a way of life. It is not a sin that it comes to us. It is a sin that we fail to resist this mood.

Now you and I need and yearn for Sunday morning. It is the day of a clean and restored heart. It is the day that even with your broken spirit you are able, with the limp in your life, to sing the Doxology. Sunday is the day we can say humbly that life is good as it is given to us. "Create in me a clean heart, o God, and put a new and right spirit within me. The sacrifice acceptable to God is a broken spirit, not a cynical spirit, not a bitter spirit. You will not reject a humble and repentant heart, o God."

Josie Jordan, a member of the congregation, wrote to me in response. First, she described the relevance of accidie in understanding her personal, social and theological dilemma. Secondly, she said that for the first time she had a word to define the last years of her father's life. Josie wrote:

Hearing these words was like having someone step inside my soul and describe the most arduous struggle I wage as I attempt to carry my concern into the wider world. On the one hand, I see the pain of those around me. The long litany of social problems comes with faces that grab hold of my heart. I put myself in the shoes of the homeless with no safe place to go. At that first second of snuggling in my warm bed, I think about those who are sleeping on the grates or in smelly shelters that night. It's not uncommon for me to cry over the Metro page or weep at the local TV news.

Personally, I've faced my own limits of compassion when helping the homeless in my neighborhood, as I have been awakened at midnight by banging on my door and demands for money. I became scared for my family and retreated to noninvolvement.

With the veil of idealism lifted I am left with an often-bitter reality. I see fundamental flaws in governmental programs on the one hand, and the limits of individual acts of kindness on the other. I'm left in an existential dilemma, caught between passionate caring and total impotence, feeling despair.

To face this reality seems more than I can bear. It is easier to look away, cross the street, stop listening to the dialogue. I shrug off the dilemma, say it's not important, and withdraw into the comforts of life. Sociologists describe this behavior as necessary group differentiation. Psychologists suggest it is accepting our limitations. Politicians insist it is facing facts. Theologians call it sin.

More often than not, falling into sin is initially quite comfortable for me. I miss the mark because I don't want to do what is required to hit it. However, as I disengage, the meaning of my life ebbs away. The cocoon of comfort that I worked so hard to construct becomes an empty shell. In protecting myself from despair, I lose the ability to rejoice. My soul forgets how to sing and my mood turns grey. Life itself becomes a chore, rather than a gift, and God becomes a concept. I have fallen into the grip of accidie.

My Dad was a high school English teacher who enjoyed his work for many years. He loved literature and music, had a terrific sense of humor, and was very well liked by his colleagues. His marriage to my mother was based on both intellectual and every-day companionship and produced three healthy, smart, and attractive daughters of whom he was proud. Being a schoolteacher his income was modest, but it was a significant step up from his childhood as a poor Irish-Catholic kid. Besides, education was his primary value. He had put himself through Brown University in the middle of the Depression and believed in education and the arts passionately.

The summer of 1961 was one of the highest points of his life. He had just been awarded a John Hay Fellowship, granting him a year's sabbatical from teaching to study at the University of California, Berkeley. We lived in a tiny town outside Hartford, Connecticut, and my father had never been west of Milwaukee, Wisconsin. The fellowship paid for the whole family to move to California for a year. This was the opportunity of a lifetime.

Two weeks before we were to leave for California, my parents traveled across Connecticut to visit a friend in the hospital. On the way home my father lost control of the car, crossed the center strip, and hit another car. He had not been speeding or drinking—he had inexplicably lost control of the wheel and had no memory of what happened. Three days later a young woman from the other car died.

My father's life crumbled with this news. His life, as he knew it, was swept away. His guilt was crushing and, indeed, something would be amiss if it were not. He could not forgive himself, nor accept forgiveness from others, for being at fault and causing the death of another, but despite my mother's desperate urging, he would not seek counseling. He was of a generation for whom seeing a psychologist or psychiatrist meant you were "crazy." Nearly forty years later, it is easy to imagine that he became clinically depressed over this event, but I haven't the expertise to determine this. I do know that he plunged into spiritual depression.

For weeks after the accident my father walked aimlessly around the house mumbling, "Why didn't God stop the car? Why did God let the cars hit?" No amount of talking with my mother could help him past this understanding of God's power in our lives, and he couldn't reconcile it with the reality he faced. He felt bitterly betrayed by God, stopped attending church and turned away from his faith. As far as he was concerned, God had abandoned him and he had no use for God. My father was never the same.

Even as a child of eight years old, I knew I'd lost my father that summer. Between his terrible guilt and the loss of his faith, he became but a shell of who he had been. He began drinking to numb his horrible mental anguish and, with each martini he drank, his joie de vivre drained away. Even when he did attend to the family, he was often irritable and impatient. Life became a living hell for him, and I overheard him murmur, "I want to die, I just want to die," on several occasions. Nine years after the accident he died of a heart attack. For years I thought he died of a broken heart. Now, I know he died of a broken spirit.

It is easy to get mired in the difficult parts of our life stories. Our dreams are not working out, yet we hold onto them. It is too frightening to let go of them because they are the foundation of our lives. We hang onto our anger because it is better than letting go and falling into the abyss of the unknown. Without letting go of dead dreams, we cannot mourn their loss. Over time, our anger congeals into resentment. Beneath the anger and resentment is sadness beyond sorrow that brings us to the brink of a broken spirit and accidie.

I measure every grief I meet
with analytic eyes;
I wonder if it weighs like mine,
Or has an easier size.

I wonder if they bore it long,
Or did it just begin?
I could not tell the date of mine
It feels so old a pain.

I wonder if it hurts to live,
And if they have to try,

And whether could they choose between,
They would not rather die.

—Emily Dickinson

When Dante descends to the Fifth Circle of the Inferno in *The Divine Comedy*, he finds there a black and loathsome marsh made by the dark waters of the Stygian stream pouring into it. There, in the putrid swamp, he sees the souls of those whom anger has ruined. They are hitting, tearing and maiming one another in ceaseless, senseless rage. But there are others there, the Master tells him, whom he cannot see, whose sobs make bubbles that rise to the surface. Who are these others and how are they ruined by anger? Dante writes:

> Fixed in the slime, they say: "Sullen were we in the sweet air, that is gladdened by the sun, carrying lazy smoke within our hearts, now lie we sullen here in the black mire." This hymn they gurgle in their throats, for they cannot speak in full words.

> *Boredom is a vital problem for the moralist, since at least half the sins of mankind are caused by the fear of it.*
>
> —*Bertrand Russell*

Dante is describing people drowning in the condition of accidie. His powerful words provide us with an early and clear portrayal of how we become mired in the muck of life, as well as what happens to us once we get stuck there. Claiming unbroken sullenness and willful gloom as key elements to getting "fixed in the slime," Dante declares that people in this condition can't even speak but are left to "gurgle."

Losing our dreams happens in two ways: mirror-shattering events or foundation-eroding experiences. Whether quick or slow, these losses have in common a wounding of our core identity stemming from the loss of our basic vision of how our life is going to go for us. We have worked hard, dreamed hard and played hard, fought hard, and many times our story has not turned out like the planned script.

We have believed in our government, fought for our country, and worshipped in our synagogues, mosques, and churches only to find that these institutions have clay feet. We have devoted ourselves to family, marriage, children, and the pursuit of the good life only to discover that the living reality is considerably more limited than our idyllic dreams. Every one of us who has given our all will, at some point, find ourselves disappointed, despairing of the outcome, and bone weary.

The weariness of which I speak is beneath the normal weariness of a hard day in field, factory, office or home. It is a weariness of the heart without hope for what is to become. We see this weariness on our faces from time to time when we stare into the mirror. We recognize the look in the subway and the office and even at the ballpark. It is the look that reveals how difficult living can be, and how we wish we could find a haven where we wouldn't ache anymore, where the weariness would be taken away, where we could stop holding our breath and exhale.

"Accidie" (*Ak-sah-dee*) and also "acedia" (*ah-see-dee-ah*) come from the Greek word, *akedos,* which refers to those who didn't care enough to bury the dead on the battlefield. These are people who had the passion for the battle but became indifferent afterward. Accidie was translated in the Middle Ages by its symptoms, sloth or torpor. But these symptoms inadequately describe the root meaning of this potent word that refers to spiritual dryness or spiritual suicide. In its fullest meaning, accidie refers to the loss of joy or faith in the goodness of life or the goodness of God.

Accidie is the evil of indifference and boredom. It leaves one passionless, apathetic and with no spice for life. It is the root of many other deadlier evils. Fleming believed accidie to be the most persistent and insidious evil of his life. In the modern world accidie is found in corporate and marital burnout, lust-driven affairs, indulgent material consumption, overeating and drinking, disillusionment in pursuit of stock market profits, ennui and social indifference. By examining the place of accidie among the traditional seven deadly sins, and by pinpointing accidie as the prime motivator of deadly evils that seek to bring power and passion into spiritually depleted lives, we open new avenues for the dialogue concerning evil in our time.

Our grandmothers and grandfathers had a particular order to these seven sins: Pride, envy, anger, accidie (usually described as sloth), covetousness, gluttony and lust. Accidie is the pivotal sin in the middle of the seven. Viewed developmentally we understand this sequence as follows. Pride is our innate desire to have the world as we want it to satisfy our needs and wants. But not long into life we are shown that it will not be just our way. Still filled with pride, we look around in envy of what others have and are certain that we should have it also. But still the world does not always give us what our pride tells us we need, and we grow deeply resentful and are filled with the life force called anger. The stage is set. Our pride, envy and anger do not give us the power or possessions or relationships or dreams or missions that propelled us. Then we slide into the muck and mire of feeling disappointment coupled with sadness and grief. Our spirit seems to have slipped from us. We are beyond the energy for anger and are filled with lethargy. Our voices gurgle in the muck. Our passion is gone. We have no fight left in us. We see nothing good in life or in the God whom we thought would protect, provide and care for us. Our soul is filled with accidie. But we are not dead and our pride urges us on. Insisting that we will not surrender, we turn to those things that ineffectually give us a sense of life, passion and power. We turn to venues that put spice in our lives: covetousness, gluttony and lust. Covetousness fills us with the passion of acquiring the material possessions our neighbor has. Gluttony attempts to fill the emptiness of our soul by turning constantly toward the refrigerator. Lust is the passion that attempts to fill emptiness with the intense sexual connection of bodily sparks, but not necessarily, with love.

Six of the deadlier evils listed by Ian Fleming are born from accidie for the same purposes as were covetousness, gluttony and lust. They were born to counter this spiritual deadness. With a loss of faith in God, we make ourselves our own god and claim our own power. Therefore, accidie is the root of cruelty, malice, snobbery, self-righteousness, hypocrisy, and avarice. When a person confronts accidie, he or she faces a pivotal spiritual crossroads where the choice reflects moral courage or moral cowardice.

There are three roads that one might take at the crossroads of accidie.

The first is the road of the broken, humbled, forgiven sinner. This person is strong enough to surrender and to grieve dreams of an idealized world. To grieve and surrender is to gain the possibility of moving forth with a balanced perspective, mindful of life's possibilities and aware of life's limitations, a posture of mature differentiation. Such a posture is one that lets God be God, neighbor be neighbor, and self be self. It is a posture that approximates the passage from James that says, "God yearns jealously for the spirit that he has made to dwell in us." Or, the Psalmist's declaration:

> The sacrifice acceptable to God is a broken spirit;
> a broken and contrite heart, O God, you will not despise.

—Psalm 51:17

You'll find a classic example of accidie in the story of Elijah in I Kings, chapters 18 and 19. Elijah had triumphed over the priests of Baal but was pursued by Queen Jezebel's headhunters. Sitting under a broom tree, Elijah begins to doubt the goodness and mercy of God and to view himself as a failure. But Yahweh is not as impressed with Elijah's sense of failure as Elijah is impressed with his own zealousness and omnipotent indispensability.

Both of these passages acknowledge a gracious, compassionate God who holds us as sacred, even as we admit that our dreams have been shattered. This is the road taken by the prodigal son *(Luke 15: 11-32)* who returns home, acknowledging his pride, willfulness, anger and covetousness. He is seeking forgiveness and restoration in the family. Forgiveness is a form of grieving because forgiveness is giving up the hope of a different past.

The second road out of accidie is the road of prideful sainthood, the choice of the older brother in the parable. Those who choose this posture do not surrender the idealized view that the world can be made as perfect as they want it to be. Instead, they believe they can make it happen by their own saintly behavior. They refuse to be broken. They refuse to grieve and walk humbly with God. They will act, instead, as their own god or they will create a fantasy hero, like James Bond, who will sustain the dream.

The third choice at the crossroads of accidie is the choice of evil. It is the prideful choice made by the angels Satan and Beelzebub as they rebelled with their forces against God, as Milton describes the mythic drama in *Paradise Lost*. Satan, filled with prideful idealization, vows eternal war against his Eternal Foe, God, rather than bend his knee and surrender. He claims all the power he needs, even if it means that he remains in deep despair or accidie. In this posture, we try to become a law unto ourselves, God. All of the evils incarnated in the nefarious characters pursued by 007 are as isolated and power-hungry as Satan.

Ian Fleming repeatedly used the ancient Christian term "accidie" to define his own personal spiritual dilemma and that of James Bond, as well as that of the key evil characters he created. Throughout the series, when Bond or the characters he fights confess their motivation, they are reflecting accidie. Fleming, who had training in Adlerian psychology, and who did extensive psychological research on megalomania and other psychological conditions, might have chosen only psychological language. But he did not. He chose spiritual language. He chose the ancient Christian theological term, accidie. He does not refer to depression and references melancholy only once when describing the condition of Tracey, Bond's wife-to-be. Interestingly, James Bond suggests that she consider the church as one place to turn for help. The word "boredom" is used occasionally, but it comes as a descriptive symptom like sloth, indifference or torpor.

The tales of James Bond reflect the isolation of individuals who have, like the angel Satan, put all their passion into denying the goodness of God and life. Many of the villains in Fleming's books could have been called Mr. No! The tales are parables about evil people who respond with moral cowardice and choose isolation and prideful self-control and power through cruelty, malice, snobbery, self-righteousness, hypocrisy, and avarice. In the Bond tales, three specific agents of Satan confess accidie as their besetting sin: Mr. Big, Dr. No, and Blofeld.

Fleming's Parables About Accidie: 1. Live And Let Die

Fleming's second tale was tentatively titled *The Undertaker's Wind*, a metaphor for one of Jamaica's two prevailing winds. In the novel renamed *Live and Let Die*, a sinister black hoodlum called Mr. Big practices Voodoo and finances the Soviet espionage operation in the Caribbean region. As well as racketeering in Harlem, Mr. Big runs a fish business in Florida as a cover for smuggling pirate treasure into the USA from Jamaica.

Mr. Big's full name is Buonaparte Ignace Gallia. These initials form his familiar name and describe his physical size, as well as his omnipotent pride in managing his underworld forces. Born half Negro and half French in Haiti, he is no ordinary criminal. He has projected his Voodoo skills into mythic power until some believe that he is a Zombie, virtually a Prince of Darkness, Satan alive in the world. This brilliant stratagem holds thousands of his employees and agents in the grip of fear, completely under his control.

Bond's first look at the awesome Mr. Big is under less than desirable circumstances. He is Mr. Big's prisoner and gazes on a man who looks as if he comes from beyond the grave with ashen, grey-black skin and a bald, round head that is twice normal size. His steady, piercing eyes are so wide-set that it is impossible to focus on both at one time. In the room where Bond encounters Mr. Big is a Voodoo effigy of the God of the Cemeteries and Chief of the Legion of the Dead, Baron Samedi. In reflecting on his life to the captured Bond, Mr. Big actually confesses that he is "prey to what the early Christians called 'accidie'." He has fallen into this spiritual lethargy not because he has been defeated, Mr. Big declares, but because he has been supremely successful in his evil craft. He stands at the pinnacle of his profession and nothing is left to enliven his days. In desperation, he tells Bond, his sole focus now is a bizarrely artistic attention to forms of malice and cruelty. Read the chilling passage and you won't soon forget this evil pathway from the crossroads of accidie.

Fleming's Parables About Accidie: 2. Dr. No

April 23 is the day some faith communities and countries celebrate the life of St. George, the patron saint of England. Whoever he was, a shameful manipulator or a heroic savior, St. George has come to represent bravery by the strong on behalf of the weak, a patron of those who risk their lives in honorable struggles with a steadfast and brave heart.

Dr. No is Fleming's retelling of the ancient story of St. George, the dragon, and the rescue of the fair maiden. The story unfolds as our brave hero is sent to search a small island where two of his countrymen have disappeared. Our hero and his assistant encounter a lovely maiden who tells them that the island they are searching is inhabited by an evil dragon she had seen on a night when the moon was full.

Bond attempts to convince the young maiden that there are no dragons, but she persists. The next day, the dragon appears, kills the good assistant and captures our hero and the fair maiden. The dragon really is a mechanical tractor equipped with a deadly flame-thrower. Bond and the maiden are taken into the den of the true dragon, the evil designer of this killing monster, Dr. No. The pride, appearance and isolation of Dr. No match those of Satan, as he confesses that his "supreme indifference" has led to his mania for the power to completely control his world. He wants to be a god, and thus, beyond human vulnerability.

Dr. No is a brilliant caricature of a mad scientist with utter disregard for persons and a maniacal determination to establish himself as sovereign. Dr. No tells his captured victims of changing his name to Julius, the name of his father who was a Methodist missionary, and No, as a rejection of his father and of all authority. He explains that he entered medical school with the express purpose of learning all that was necessary to be secure from physical weakness. He claims God's power and, in his cosmos, all persons are as insignificant as bugs under a scientist's microscope. Bond's own courage and endurance are measured in a gauntlet of extremes that Dr. No has constructed.

In the end, of course, Bond survives and Dr. No, a scientific dragon, is killed. Thank you, St. George, for saving another maiden and showing us another departure from the crossroads of accidie.

Fleming's Parables About Accidie: 3. You Only Live Twice

James Bond marries only once in Fleming's tales, but his wife is killed by Bond's arch-enemy, Blofeld, on the day of their wedding. Bond begins to lose his edge. He deals with his loss the way men often do: drinking, eating too much, gambling, and losing his sense of mission. His boss, M, has Bond examined by a neurologist, who reports that Bond is in shock and deep grief, and his behavior is quite appropriate. Read the fascinating passage early in *You Only Live Twice* in which the neurologist reports on Bond's condition. You may be surprised that his diagnosis for Bond's departure from accidie is not more rest. Rather, the expert's advice is that Bond should be given an impossible job.

Accidie is the heart of the dragon without passion, spirit or vitality. Its blood is cool, fostering indifference, carelessness, boredom and cynicism about life and God.

Bond has a choice. Does he succumb to his own accidie or accept the impossible job of slaying the dragon of Despair? Bond accepts the impossible job. He sets off again in pursuit of the demonic Blofeld who, like the Devil, has reincarnated himself for a third time in the figure of Shatterhand in *You Only Live Twice*. Appearing as a modern version of Dante's Giant Despair, he offers free death by suicide at his Castle of Death. In this old-fashioned morality tale, the Devil of Despair once again lives in isolation with death. In this story, Bond is not only rescuing the fair maiden, the pert Kissy Suzuki; he also is rescuing himself from his own wish to die from his despair. Wearing a black silk kimono across which a golden dragon is sprawled, Blofeld as Shatterhand delivers the ultimate apologia for accidie. Like Mr. Big, Blofeld actually uses the word "accidie," which he describes as "an utter boredom with the affairs of mankind." Search out this passage later in the novel. It's one of Fleming's most remarkable discourses on the deadly temptations related to accidie.

Of course, you already know what happens, even if you haven't read the novel or watched the movie version of this story. Our faith says that Life ultimately is stronger than Death. That's what Fleming, the flawed saint, preached again and again. That's why Fleming's St. George found his way beyond the crossroads of accidie in novel after novel. This is our Good News, too. The Dragon—which in its most powerful incarnation is the refusal to live and rejoice until we descend into utter indifference, carelessness, inertia and apathy toward God's creation—can be overcome. We can reclaim joy.

Moral Inventory:

As you prepare for this final moral inventory, let me share a few of my own spiritual disciplines to restore spiritual vitality. Those most helpful to me are: singing (I sing a short song of thanks each morning when I walk to retrieve the newspaper); prayer (I pray some or all of the Prayer of St. Francis … "Lord, make me an instrument…" each morning); manual labor (since so much of my work is emotional and intellectual, I ground my mortality in manual labor); maintenance of community (I keep active with other people); grieving and gratitude (I have come to believe that intentional grieving and expressing gratitude are two crucial spiritual disciplines)—and, finally, laughter (yes, laugh out loud, too, if you want).

Reflect on these final questions:

How long has it been since you sang with great joy?

Were you ever filled with a deep and prolonged joy?

If you were joyous and are no longer so, what squelched or crushed the joy in your soul?

What feeling replaced the passion and vitality of joy?

Were you ever able to restore the sense of joy and, if so, how did you do it?

Study Guide

Our Lives Have Been Shaken — And Stirred.
Let's Try to Put Them Back on Solid Ground.

Every now and then, when we least expect it, the world grabs our minds, shakes our bones, stirs our souls, then demands a response from our hearts. These cataclysmic events usually start with jolting news: Our doctor says, "You have cancer…" Or, a spouse says, "I want a divorce…" Or, the call comes, "Your father has died." Or, the newscast heralds a tragic death on the world stage.

One such poignant event occurs in the Bible with the announcement:

> In the year that King Uzziah died, I saw the Lord sitting on a throne … Seraphs were in attendance above him … And I said: "Woe is me! I am lost, for I am a man of unclean lips, and I live among a people of unclean lips; yet my eyes have seen the King, the Lord of hosts!" Then I heard the voice of the Lord saying, "Whom shall I send, and who will go for us?" And I said, "Here am I; send me!"

It's a passage in *Isaiah 6* that is as relevant for our personal and communal life today as it was more than 2,500 years ago.

On September 11, 2001, surely our lives were shaken and stirred. The events of that day seared our souls, wrenched our hearts, challenged our minds, unleashed our rage, kindled our compassion and eclipsed our imagination. To form a response, we need, like Isaiah, a soul-searching assessment of ourselves as individuals, communities and nations—a spiritual and moral inventory.

Life asks the questions. Our heads, and even more importantly, our hearts, must answer. Compiling a moral and spiritual checklist first requires asking disturbing questions: How am I doing with my God? What disciplines and commitments will guide my life? What about my own evil? What are the evil forces I condone or encourage as part of my life, my community, my nation? If the world currently reflects a spiritual war between the forces of good and evil, on which side of the rampart do I stand?

Good and evil, in all their manifestations, have permeated the human imagination since the snake slithered through the garden of Adam and Eve. Throughout history, tales abound of heroic warriors combating malevolent forces bent on corrupting and destroying our world. But, for most of us in the real world, the choices are rarely between a warrior of light and a demon. Our lives are full of ambiguity.

I suggest two texts to guide our spiritual and moral inventory. The first is not surprising, since *The Letter of James* is a part of the Christian Bible—a religious text read by billions. But the truth is that this letter is full of surprises—closer to the world of secular ethics than theological discourse. The second is the adventures of James Bond. A fictional creation of British writer Ian Fleming, Bond appears an unlikely candidate to provide moral guidance. As implausible as it sounds, however, moral and theological undercurrents pulse through each of Fleming's James Bond novels, posing a classical Christian view of God and the Devil and the mythic spiritual war between the forces of Light and Darkness.

The Letter of James and the James Bond tales provide a moral compass against which we can conduct our personal-and-communal, moral-and-spiritual inventory. Both are relevant for our time and the two together shine a very bright light on each other and on us. Depending on your personality, this may feel more like an intellectual exercise or it may very well become an examination of the heart.

Join me on this pilgrimage.

Practical Suggestions

Based on my years of working with individuals, couples, groups and congregations, here are suggestions for using this book:

Start wherever you are. You may have chosen the book because you are an avid James Bond fan. As such, you may have opened this book hoping to find some new perspective on the Bond tales. If you hang in with me I suspect strongly that you will emerge with a new point of view. Maybe you are a dedicated pilgrim eager to conduct an intense personal inventory. Whether as a private reader, a member of a small group of 8 to 12 searching pilgrims, or of a class of numerous members, you will come with different personal needs and preferences for such an experience. So, choose formats that work best for you. Perhaps it's intellectual curiosity—or perhaps it's more. You may be facing an ethical or spiritual crisis that demands that you surrender yourself to a personal, transforming inventory. Or you may not know why you are venturing into this process but you are open to a change of mind, heart and soul. I invite you all to join the Bond journey.

- **This is not a book limited to Christians.** I could demonstrate that the James Bond tales are more theologically rooted in Christianity than *The Letter of James* itself. But, you may be reading this book as a Jew and, if so, my hope is that it will make you a better Jew. If you're Muslim, a better Muslim. If Buddhist, a better Buddhist—and so on. If you're agnostic, perhaps you'll emerge as a person of clearer mind and heart about what is important to you.

- **This book works best if you come with an open heart and mind.** In the last fifteen years that I practiced as a pastoral counselor, I gave to each couple who came for counseling a copy of the prayer of St. Francis: "Lord,

make me an instrument of thy peace, where there is
hatred, let me sow love..." I gave this prayer to believers
and unbelievers, Jews, Christians and agnostics because,
in spite of its Christian origin, it is not just a Christian
prayer. I suggested that each person pray the prayer every
day for 90 days, individually and as a couple, with special
focus on that portion of the prayer that prays:
"O Divine Master, grant that I may not so much seek
to be consoled as to console, to be understood as to
understand, to be loved as to love." Some folks never
looked at the prayer but there were some who took the
task very seriously. One powerful Capitol Hill couple
took it so seriously that even when they were continents
apart they would call each night and pray the prayer
together. The impact was dramatic. At one of our
sessions, the highly competitive man who had spent years
attempting to force his wife and everyone else on Capitol
Hill to understand him, sat weeping as he shared the
transformation that for the first time in his life he was
seeking more to understand his wife than forcing her to
understand him. The "instrument" prayer is about shifting
our internal vision of self and our world. This guidebook is
offered in the same spirit.

- **Covenant for confidentiality.** This is a guideline familiar
  to millions of people who are veterans of small-group
  study. If you use this book as a workbook in which you
  write personal journal passages, be sure that what you
  write is kept private. If you are in a small group (8-12) or
  a class of many, covenant together that what is said in the
  room stays in the room. Even your spouse doesn't need to
  hear what someone else reveals.

- **The pace is yours to set.** Some people are capable of a
  daily schedule of personal examination and prayer. I am
  not! Although most mornings I do sing the doxology on
  my trek to fetch the paper at the end of the driveway, and
  I do pray at least some portion of the Francis "instrument"
  prayer each morning, I am not a daily Bible reader, a
  meditation prayer, a journal writer. I am a gulper. I read

large passages of the Bible at one time. I read novels and other writers to challenge my soul and transform my heart and mind. I do more self examination while working in my garden or my woodshop than I would ever do attempting a journal or a meditation process. That's who I am. That's what works for me. I attempt to open myself to be receptive to the surprises that come to me constantly on the slant and occasionally hit me right between my eyeballs. Each of us must adapt according to our needs and our capabilities.

- **Everyone needs a copy of this book.** Each chapter in the book contains discussion-sparking questions and points for reflection. Even couples, if they participate in a weekly class, will appreciate having their own individual copy.

- **Compare English-language versions of the Bible.** In this book, biblical passages come from the King James Version. For clarity in understanding passages—and to enliven class discussion—bring other translations of key passages to share.

- **Invite members of your group to divide up Fleming's novels.** This is one of the really fun parts in this study! Your homework is reading James Bond novels! Invite individuals each to pick one or two Bond novels they will read—and become your group's resident "expert" on novels.

And now, it's 10:00! Do you know where your Devil is?

Ultimately, Fleming's novels and the adventure in this book are about looking at our lives in fresh ways.

So, have you looked in the mirror lately and examined the Devil looking at you? One way to begin this process is to read scripture formatively, that is, with your heart as if the scripture was written only for you, not exegetically, that is with your mind.

Each chapter in this book begins with a scriptural quotation, usually from *The Letter of James*. I invite you to read it formatively. This kind of reading, sometimes referred to as *Lectio Divina*, is really a form of prayer that's at least 1,000 years old. It's one of the world's venerable spiritual disciplines, which are resurfacing in our modern world, thank goodness, along with the deadlier sins that concerned Fleming and concern us today.

So, what are you waiting for? Get started on our adventure!

Bond Movies vs. Novels

I admit that I'm a lit snob, but I also do enjoy movies of all sorts. When books become films, however, I usually miss the subtle intricacies of the prose. That's especially true in the action-packed Bond genre.

In *Quantum of Solace*, for example, watch what the filmmakers did with the structure of the original story in which Fleming seats Bond in a chintzy, too-soft couch—and our man of action never moves! In this short tale by Fleming, Bond enjoys a drink and listens to a tale of a decayed marriage turned bitterly foul. It's wonderful prose, but a cinematic challenge.

Dr. No was the first full-length movie made from a Bond tale. However, Fleming never fully recovered from an earlier heart attack and had very little influence on this film version. *Dr. No*, *Goldfinger* and the 2006 version of *Casino Royale* are the closest remakes of the original tales and each of them varies in numerous ways. Many 007 movies have little in common with the original Fleming tale other than the title.

You may be wondering: Can I accomplish this Bible study by simply watching the movies? No, you'll be lost in the course of this discussion. There is original creativity in the films, but not Ian Fleming's creativity for the most part. That's why this Study Guide recommends an unusual strategy for small groups: Ask each participant to read one or two different Fleming books in the course of your study. That way, you'll turn your group members into resident experts on the original tales.

I realize that the Bond movies are the primary windows into Bond's world for millions of men and women. So, I encourage you to talk about this issue of the variances between books and films, which may help point you toward some of the enduring greatness of Fleming's work. To get you started, I am going to share a few of my own notes on two films.

We've made it easy for you to join this part of the discussion. Look for the link to "Movies vs. Novels" at our Web site: www.BondBibleStudy.info

Movies vs. Novels: *Casino Royale* (2006 version)

I've watched this movie three times and enjoyed it each time, although the hyperactivity bores me after a while. The movie uses the novel's core story but updates and changes it in countless ways.

Daniel Craig is my choice as the best Bond. Put his photo next to a picture of the musician and actor, Hoagy Carmichael, who was Fleming's prototype of Bond, and you have twins.

Judi Dench is a fabulous choice as M for many reasons. Many fans thinks M is modeled after Admiral Godfrey, Fleming's boss during WW II, but M is the name Fleming used for his strong-willed mother.

The blood oozing from Le Chiffre's eye is a marvelous touch. One of the characteristics of the Devil is a red eye. Note Red Grant's eye in *From Russia With Love*.

Overall, this film is darker than Fleming's own bleak view of the world. Even Mathis, Bond's fellow French agent in the book, is a skunk in the movie. Read the novel and then watch this film and you'll find many other details faithfully transferred onto the screen, even the chair on which Bond is tortured! There are also many differences. Help us list more of these.

Movies vs. Novels: *Goldfinger*

Once again, we've got Fleming's core story with a lot of hype. The novel offers considerably more depth, but the movie cuts out so much dialogue that the philosophical and theological language is lost. A couple of lines from Goldfinger's confessional speech remain in the film.

One serious discussion between Bond and Goldfinger underscores that Goldfinger's motivation for detonating an atomic bomb in Ft. Knox is to cause "economic chaos in the West." Shades of the attacks on Sept. 11, 2001!

The hit song that we all remember from this film underscores the connection with Midas, which I have discussed in this book.

We hope you'll add your own thoughts on "Movies vs. Novels" to our Web site: www.BondBibleStudy.info

Ian Fleming Chronology

1908 Ian Fleming is born May 28 to Valentine and Evelyn St. Croix Rose Fleming. Ian is the second son, ten months younger than his life-long rival, Peter. Michael, who later would die of wounds as a prisoner of war after Dunkirk, and Richard, would follow Ian as brothers in this wealthy, socially prominent Scottish family. The family's large home, a Gothic palace, sits on a wooded paradise at Ipsden, Oxfordshire.

Valentine is described as temperate, cautious, honorable, kind and dutiful to society. Evelyn is extravagant, beautiful, passionate, strong willed, demanding, a law unto herself.

Peter, age 8, and Ian, age 7, are sent to Durnford, a boarding school famous for its Spartan methods and for bullying new students. Ian is scarred by this experience and remained cautious of anyone who attempts to get close to him for the rest of his life.

1917 Valentine Fleming is killed on May 20 on a WWI battlefield. Valentine's obituary, printed in the London Times, is written by Winston Churchill, a fellow Conservative MP. Peter, Ian, Richard and Michael mature under the dominating control of their mother and the idealized memory of their war-hero father.

1921 Ian enrolls at Eton. His sentiments for Eton are captured fully in a gift Ian would present late in his life to the Old Etonian Golfing Society. The silver trophy called the James Bond Vase is in the shape of a large silver chamber pot.

Peter, first born and old beyond his years, assumes the duties as head of the family with excessive seriousness at Eton. Ian no longer competes with his brother scholastically; he chooses athletics.

Ian will not graduate from Eton. He leaves under a dark cloud of pending expulsion involving a car and girls. Ian's mother withdraws him and sends him to a highly disciplined Prussian-style military school.

1926 Ian is enrolled at the Royal Military College, Sandhurst, England. It is Hell for Cadet Fleming who spends most of his time on the square being knocked into shape by the drill masters. He responds poorly in his subjects and expends minimal effort. He seems past caring. His spirit for life has been drained from him. Ian is confined to barracks for six months when caught climbing into the college after a rendezvous with a girl in London. His stay lasts one year, and he leaves the school full of bitterness and resentment.

Fleming does not graduate from Eton or Sandhurst. He has many girlfriends during these years. He is known for regaling them with adventurous tales. He loves rich foods, elegant automobiles and eccentric clothing. He is a dandy, a born actor. Ian falls in love with a young woman named Peggy. When Peggy honors an earlier commitment and goes to a dance with another man, Ian sleeps with another woman and contracts gonorrhea.

1927 Ian is sent to a private tutor at Kitzbuhel, Switzerland.

Ian's mother, exasperated by her son's failures, sends him to a Scottish former diplomat and spy, tutor Ernan Forbes-Dennis and his Quaker wife, novelist Phyllis Bottome, who was Adler's official biographer. Under their tutelage at Tennerhof, Ian becomes a reader of good literature as well as a student of Adlerian psychology. He makes his first real attempt at writing literature at age 19.

Later in life, Fleming would describe this period as "that time when the sun always shone." Forbes-Dennis and Bottome nurture him. In addition to providing an emotionally safe and nurturing environment, they help him find direction and purpose for his life, directing his study for the Foreign Service Exam. No longer under the direct influence of his mother and family, Fleming delves into the great books of Europe and the required books for a London University degree. He becomes fluent in German, French and useable Russian.

After Tennerhof, Ian resides in Geneva and becomes engaged to Monique Panchaud de Bottomes, a young, amusing French-Swiss Protestant. When their engagement crumbles, partly due to his mother's objections, Fleming boasts that he plans to become "quite bloody-minded about women from now on."

1931 Fleming becomes Reuters's correspondent in Moscow covering the trial of several British engineers accused of spying in Stalin's Russia. Fleming's accounts of the trial often surpass his fellow correspondents' in speed and imagination. His fanciful articles make events appear more dramatic than they are in reality.

1935 Fleming commissions Percy Muir to amass a collection of 19th- and 20th-Century first-edition books that "started something" or "made things happen." The Fleming Collection becomes so valuable that it is protected at Oxford during WW II and is now housed in the Lilly Library of the University of Indiana.

Prior to the war, Fleming talks about his awful boredom and specifically about accidie. His dark melancholy destroys his relationships with women.

1939 In the spring, prior to entering Naval Intelligence officially, Ian returns to Moscow as part of a Trade Delegation. Actually, he is sent as a spy.

On July 26, 1939, Fleming is appointed a lieutenant in the Royal Naval Volunteer Reserve and is recruited to be Assistant to the Director of Naval Intelligence. His boss, Rear Admiral John H. Godfrey, is believed by many to be Fleming's model for M, James Bond's boss in the 007 tales. Fleming's skills are "running things" and drafting memoirs with precision and clarity. He was a "skilled fixer," employing tact and charm with a little imagination added for spice. To say that he is a personal assistant does not capture the power and scope of his position. From the beginning, Godfrey places exceptional trust in Ian and arranges for him to be shown every detail of the operation.

1941 In June, Fleming accompanies Godfrey on a secret mission, via Lisbon, to Washington, DC, where they meet with Herbert Hoover and "Wild" Bill Donovan, Director of the newly forming OSS. In Lisbon, Fleming fantasizes a gambling experience in which he wins so much money from his Nazi opponents that he strikes a blow to the enemy. This fanciful idea later becomes the basis for the game in *Casino Royale*. In reality, Fleming plays against some Portuguese businessmen and loses all his money.

From Room 39 at Whitehall, Fleming directs the No. 30 Assault
Unit, which he calls "My Red Indians." It is an excellent commando
unit serving as "Intelligence Scavengers." Near the end of the war,
the Red Indians capture German naval archives.

1944 In autumn, Fleming makes an official trip to Washington
and on to Jamaica. He loves the island and decides to live the rest
of his life there. Through his friend Ivar Bryce, Fleming buys 14
acres on the North Shore at Oracabessa. He calls it Goldeneye. His
neighbor, Noel Coward, teases Fleming constantly about his house
calling it "Golden Eye, Nose and Throat." It is here that all the
James Bond tales are written.

1945 Fleming is discharged from the Navy and becomes
Foreign Manager of Kemsley Newspapers where he is responsible
for building one of the most substantial organizations in the news
business, the Mercury Service. When the Mercury Service begins
to founder, he was passed over for advancement and feels the pinch
financially. A second son, he receives no inheritance. His life is
stalled, so he decides to marry for the first time. During this period
he adopts his costume: blue polka-dot tie, black moccasins, and a
dark blue suit. Ian smokes 70 cigarettes and consumes a quarter
bottle of gin a day.

1952 Fleming marries Ann Charteris at Goldeneye in Jamaica.
Noel Coward is the witness. Ann, now in her third marriage,
has divorced her second husband, Esmond, the second Viscount
Rothermer. The Flemings' only child, Caspar Robert, is born August,
1952.

1953 *Casino Royale* is published April 13 in England.

1954 *Live and Let Die*

1955 *Moonraker*

1956 *Diamonds are Forever*

1957 *From Russia, With Love*

1958 *Dr. No*

1959 *Goldfinger*

1960 *For Your Eyes Only*

1961 *Thunderball* is published and, that same year, *LIFE* magazine lists the 10 favorite books of President John Kennedy, including *From Russia with Love*. This spurs Fleming's sales and, later that year, producers Harry Saltzman and Albert Broccoli take options on all Bond novels for film production.

1962 *The Spy Who Loved Me*

1963 *On Her Majesty's Secret Service*

1964 *You Only Live Twice* and *Chitty Chitty Bang Bang*

1964 Ian Lancaster Fleming dies August 12 of a heart attack suffered while attending a committee meeting at the Royal St. George Golf Club.

1965 *The Man with the Golden Gun*

1966 *Octopussy*

The Letter of James

To help you fully enjoy and appreciate the meaning of *The Letter of James*, here is an easy-to-read translation of the New Testament book as presented by the International Bible Society's new *The Books of the Bible* program. This format, which uses contemporary language and removes distracting chapter and verse markings, was developed by IBS to encourage more comprehensive Bible reading.

For more information about *The Books of The Bible*, visit www.thebooksofthebible.info.

To order a print edition of the full Bible or portions of The Books of The Bible, visit www.IBSDirect.com or call 800-524-1588.

The Books of The Bible is also available on Sony Reader.

 The Books of The Bible

James, a servant of God and of the Lord Jesus Christ,

To the twelve tribes scattered among the nations:

Greetings.

Consider it pure joy, my brothers and sisters, whenever you face trials of many kinds, because you know that the testing of your faith produces perseverance. Let perseverance finish its work so that you may be mature and complete, not lacking anything. If any of you lacks wisdom, you should ask God, who gives generously to all without finding fault, and it will be given to you. But when you ask, you must believe and not doubt, because the one who doubts is like a wave of the sea, blown and tossed by the wind. Those who doubt should not think they will receive anything from the Lord; they are double-minded and unstable in all they do.

Believers in humble circumstances ought to take pride in their high position. But the rich should take pride in their humiliation—since they will pass away like a wild flower. For the sun rises with scorching heat and withers the plant; its blossom falls and its beauty is destroyed. In the same way, the rich will fade away even while they go about their business.

Blessed are those who persevere under trial, because when they have stood the test, they will receive the crown of life that God has promised to those who love him.

When tempted, no one should say, "God is tempting me." For God cannot be tempted by evil, nor does he tempt anyone; but each of you is tempted when you are dragged away by your own evil desire and enticed. Then, after desire has conceived, it gives birth to sin; and sin, when it is full-grown, gives birth to death.

Don't be deceived, my dear brothers and sisters. Every good and perfect gift is from above, coming down from the Father of the heavenly lights, who does not change like shifting shadows. He chose to give us birth through the word of truth, that we might be a kind of firstfruits of all he created.

My dear brothers and sisters, take note of this: Everyone should be quick to listen, slow to speak and slow to become angry, because our anger does not produce the righteousness that God desires. Therefore, get rid of all moral filth and the evil that is so prevalent and humbly accept the word planted in you, which can save you.

Do not merely listen to the word, and so deceive yourselves. Do what it says. Those who listen to the word but do not do what it says are like people who look at their faces in a mirror and, after looking at themselves, go away and immediately forget what they look like. But those who look intently into the perfect law that gives freedom and continue in it—not forgetting what they have heard, but doing it—they will be blessed in what they do.

Those who consider themselves religious and yet do not keep a tight rein on their tongues deceive themselves, and their religion is worthless. Religion that God our Father accepts as pure and faultless is this: to look after orphans and widows in their distress and to keep oneself from being polluted by the world.

My brothers and sisters, believers in our glorious Lord Jesus Christ must not show favoritism. Suppose someone comes into your meeting wearing a gold ring and fine clothes, and a poor person in filthy old clothes also comes in. If you show special attention to the one wearing fine clothes and say, "Here's a good seat for you," but say to the one who is poor, "You stand there" or "Sit on the floor by my feet," have you not discriminated among yourselves and become judges with evil thoughts?

Listen, my dear brothers and sisters: Has not God chosen those who are poor in the eyes of the world to be rich in faith and to inherit the kingdom he promised those who love him? But you have dishonored the poor. Is it not the rich who are exploiting you? Are they not the ones who are dragging you into court? Are they not the ones who are blaspheming the noble name of him to whom you belong?

If you really keep the royal law found in Scripture, "Love your neighbor as yourself," you are doing right. But if you show favoritism, you sin and are convicted by the law as lawbreakers. For whoever keeps the whole law and yet stumbles at just one point is guilty of breaking all of it. For he who said, "You shall not commit adultery," also said, "You shall not murder." If you do not commit adultery but do commit murder, you have become a lawbreaker.

Speak and act as those who are going to be judged by the law that gives freedom, because judgment without mercy will be shown to anyone who has not been merciful. Mercy triumphs over judgment.

What good is it, my brothers and sisters, if people claim to have faith but have no deeds? Can such faith save them? Suppose a brother or sister is without clothes and daily food. If one of you says to them, "Go in peace; keep warm and well fed," but does nothing about their physical needs, what good is it? In the same way, faith by itself, if it is not accompanied by action, is dead.

But someone will say, "You have faith; I have deeds."

Show me your faith without deeds, and I will show you my faith by what I do. You believe that there is one God. Good! Even the demons believe that—and shudder.

You foolish person, do you want evidence that faith without deeds is useless*? Was not our father Abraham considered righteous for what he did when he offered his son Isaac on the altar? You see that his faith and his actions were working together, and his faith was made complete by what he did. And the scripture was fulfilled that says, "Abraham believed God, and it was credited to him as righteousness,"* and he was called God's friend. You see that people are justified by what they do and not by faith alone.

In the same way, was not even Rahab the prostitute considered righteous for what she did when she gave lodging to the spies and sent them off in a different direction? As the body without the spirit is dead, so faith without deeds is dead.

Not many of you should presume to be teachers, my brothers and sisters, because you know that we who teach will be judged more strictly. We all stumble in many ways. Those who are never at fault in what they say are perfect, able to keep their whole body in check.

When we put bits into the mouths of horses to make them obey us, we can turn the whole animal. Or take ships as an example. Although they are so large and are driven by strong winds, they are steered by a very small rudder wherever the pilot wants to go. Likewise, the tongue is a small part of the body, but it makes great boasts. Consider what a great forest is set on fire by a small spark. The tongue also is a fire, a world of evil among the parts of the body. It corrupts the whole person, sets the whole course of one's life on fire, and is itself set on fire by hell.

All kinds of animals, birds, reptiles and sea creatures are being tamed and have been tamed by human beings, but no one can tame the tongue. It is a restless evil, full of deadly poison.

With the tongue we praise our Lord and Father, and with it we curse human beings, who have been made in God's likeness. Out of the same mouth come praise and cursing. My brothers and sisters, this should not be. Can both fresh water and salt water flow from the same spring? My brothers and sisters, can a fig tree bear olives, or a grapevine bear figs? Neither can a salt spring produce fresh water.

Who is wise and understanding among you? Let them show it by their good life, by deeds done in the humility that comes from wisdom. But if you harbor bitter envy and selfish ambition in your hearts, do not boast about it or deny the truth. Such "wisdom" does not come down from heaven but is earthly, unspiritual, demonic. For where you have envy and selfish ambition, there you find disorder and every evil practice.

But the wisdom that comes from heaven is first of all pure; then peace-loving, considerate, submissive, full of mercy and good fruit, impartial and sincere. Peacemakers who sow in peace reap a harvest of righteousness.

What causes fights and quarrels among you? Don't they come from your desires that battle within you? You desire but do not have, so you kill. You covet but you cannot get what you want, so you quarrel and fight. You do not have because you do not ask God. When you ask, you do not receive, because you ask with wrong motives, that you may spend what you get on your pleasures.

You adulterous people, don't you know that friendship with the world means enmity against God? Anyone who chooses to be a friend of the world becomes an enemy of God. Or do you think Scripture says without reason that he jealously longs for the spirit he has caused to dwell in us? But he gives us more grace. That is why Scripture says:

> "God opposes the proud
>
> but shows favor to the humble and oppressed."

Submit yourselves, then, to God. Resist the devil, and he will flee from you. Come near to God and he will come near to you. Wash your hands, you sinners, and purify your hearts, you double-minded. Grieve, mourn and wail. Change your laughter to mourning and your joy to gloom. Humble yourselves before the Lord, and he will lift you up.

Brothers and sisters, do not slander one another. Anyone who speaks against a brother or sister or judges them speaks against the law and judges it. When you judge the law, you are not keeping it, but sitting in judgment on it. There is only one Lawgiver and Judge, the one who is able to save and destroy. But you—who are you to judge your neighbor?

Now listen, you who say, "Today or tomorrow we will go to this or that city, spend a year there, carry on business and make money." Why, you do not even know what will happen tomorrow. What is your life? You are a mist that appears for a little while and then vanishes. Instead, you ought to say, "If it is the Lord's will, we will live and do this or that." As it is, you boast in your arrogant schemes. All such boasting is evil. So then, if you know the good you ought to do and don't do it, you sin.

Now listen, you rich people, weep and wail because of the misery that is coming on you. Your wealth has rotted, and moths have eaten your clothes. Your gold and silver are corroded. Their corrosion will testify against you and eat your flesh like fire. You have hoarded wealth in the last days. Look! The wages you failed to pay the workers who mowed your fields are crying out against you. The cries of the harvesters have reached the ears of the Lord Almighty. You have lived on earth in luxury and self-indulgence. You have fattened yourselves in the day of slaughter. You have condemned and murdered the innocent one, who was not opposing you.

Be patient, then, brothers and sisters, until the Lord's coming. See how the farmer waits for the land to yield its valuable crop, patiently waiting for the autumn and spring rains. You too, be patient and stand firm, because the Lord's coming is near. Don't grumble against one another, brothers and sisters, or you will be judged. The Judge is standing at the door!

Brothers and sisters, as an example of patience in the face of suffering, take the prophets who spoke in the name of the Lord. As you know, we count as blessed those who have persevered. You have heard of Job's perseverance and have seen what the Lord finally brought about. The Lord is full of compassion and mercy.

Above all, my brothers and sisters, do not swear—not by heaven or by earth or by anything else. All you need to say is a simple "Yes" or "No." Otherwise you will be condemned.

Is anyone among you in trouble? Let them pray. Is anyone happy? Let them sing songs of praise. Is anyone among you sick? Let them call the elders of the church to pray over them and anoint them with oil in the name of the Lord. And the prayer offered in faith will make them well; the Lord will raise them up. If they have sinned, they will be forgiven. Therefore confess your sins to each other and pray for each other so that you may be healed. The prayer of a righteous person is powerful and effective.

Elijah was a human being, even as we are. He prayed earnestly that it would not rain, and it did not rain on the land for three and a half years. Again he prayed, and the heavens gave rain, and the earth produced its crops.

My brothers and sisters, if one of you should wander from the truth and someone should bring them back, remember this: Whoever turns a sinner from the way of error will save them from death and cover over a multitude of sins.

Trivia Quizzes

These questions are for your enjoyment as you learn. Some questions are easy; some are difficult. You're likely to have various levels of interest in your discussion group, so there's a little something here for everyone.

We also hope you'll play a role in the global discussion we're sparking on Fleming's spiritual wisdom. If you take issue with any of these questions or answers, please visit our Web site, www. BondBibleStudy.info, and click on the link to "Trivia Quizzes."

Perhaps you've got your own questions you want to raise. Perhaps you find ways to adapt these questions for your group's individual interests. If so, please share them with us on the Web site. We'd love to hear from you—and to acknowledge your work in helping to spread resources for this Bible Study.

To start you off, here are eight short quizzes you could sprinkle through your weeks with Fleming and Bond.

General Trivia Quiz

1. Which of Fleming's fictional cars has the license plate GEN II? Can you translate its meaning?

2. Literary critic Paul Johnson famously thrashed which Fleming novel, calling it "the nastiest book I ever read"?

3. Who is M's private secretary? Who are Bond's secretaries?

4. Bond often receives special gadgets. Who prepares these for him? What 20th century English author was known by this same nickname?

5. Who is Bond's CIA agent-compatriot and friend?

6. James Bond is called "Saint James" in at least one tale, but which saint is he called in 11 of the 14 books?

7. Which Fleming character shares Fleming's birth date, May 28, 1908?

8. Which demonic character plans to use biological warfare, including anthrax? In which novel?

9. Bond, a civil-servant secret agent, often is referred to as a spy. Actually, he is a spy in only one tale. Which one?

10. In *Thunderball*, the main enemy shifts from SMERSH to the international crime syndicate SPECTRE. Which Fleming character creates SPECTRE?

Casino Royale Quiz

1. Bond's dry martini is now a famous recipe, prepared shaken, of course. What name did Bond give this drink he invented?

2. What is the card game Bond and Le Chiffre play at Royale-les-Eaux?

3. Who kills Le Chiffre?

4. Bond's right hand is branded with a Russian symbol indicating he is a spy. This also resembles what common English letter?

5. Fleming describes Bond as looking like which famous musician, songwriter and occasional movie actor?

6. Bond is described in *Casino Royale* as having a "thick comma" of hair above which eyebrow? And a scar down which cheek?

7. Where does Bond hide the check for his gambling receipts?

8. Who does Bond describe as having no one to record his story or his parables?

Diamonds Are Forever Quiz

1. Based on the Kefauver Report in the U.S., which industry did Fleming claim was the biggest in America?

2. True or False: "Theatrical" is a term used continually in this tale as the root of hypocrisy.

3. What does Bond like shaken, not stirred?

4. Felix Leiter's car is a Studebaker with a Cadillac engine. What does he call it?

5. Bond said Las Vegas architecture was from the Gilded Mousetrap School. Why?

6. What does Bond see that makes him understand, for the first time, the point of being a millionaire?

7. One of the thugs out to kill Bond and Tiffany has a tag that says, "My Blood Group is F." What does that mean?

8. True or False: Most scholars believe the Letter of James was written by the brother of Jesus.

9. True or False: Most books in the New Testament are letters.

10. True or False: A major clue that this novel is intended as satire is the names of characters, such as Tiffany and Seraffimo.

Moonraker Quiz

1. Who is Bond's elderly Scottish housekeeper?

2. What is the model of Bond's car, wrecked in this tale, and described as vintage 1930 with a 4 ½ liter, supercharged engine?

3. When M addresses Bond as "James," what is he indicating to Bond?

4. In the early Bond tales there are two other special agents identified with 00 status. What are their numbers?

5. A prescient moment in the novel is Bond's glimpse of a road sign that says, "Shell is Here." What key letter is missing from Bond's view?

6. Sir Hugo Drax is actually Baron von Drache. What does Drache mean in German?

7. Bond wins a crucial Bridge game by dealing what?

8. After Bond and Gala Brand are nearly killed along the cliff, what is the first thing Bond does?

9. Bond plans to sacrifice himself by blowing up the Moonraker. Whose intelligence saves him by offering an alternative plan?

10. What bird does Fleming use at the beginning and end of this tale to focus Bond's spiritual reflections?

From Russia With Love Quiz

1. What does Red Grant defect from the West to become?

2. True or False: SMERSH, which means "Death to Spies," was a Fleming creation.

3. True or False: The Koklov Affair and Grubozaboyshikov, who signs the order for Bond's death, were Fleming creations.

4. Who is the coldly malicious torturer with thinning orange hair who commands SMERSH operations?

5. When 007 first appears in this tale, what is the spiritual sin from which Bond suffers?

6. What does Bond say the gods make people before they destroy them?

7. There's a duel seduction in this novel. What temptation works on M? What temptations work on Bond?

8. What does Bond walk through to view the Soviet command in Istanbul?

9. How do Bond and Tatiana depart Turkey?

10. Red Grant disguises himself as Norman Nash. In Russian, what does "Nash" mean?

11. How much blood does the human body contain?

12. This tale ends with Bond near death. In *Dr. No*, what is his recovery called?

Goldfinger Quiz

1. Fleming loves to play with names. In Latin, what is the meaning of Goldfinger's first name, Auric?

2. Goldfinger's ugly appearance resembles which mythological king?

3. What is the disguise behind which Junius DuPont, who asks Bond's assistance in stopping Goldfinger's card sharking, hopes to cover his shame as an American millionaire?

4. Why does Bond feel disgusted and ashamed after eating the finest meal ever with DuPont?

5. What book does Bond use to hide his Walther PPK?

6. Which saint is Bond quoting when he pleads, "Oh Lord, give me chastity. But don't give it yet!"

7. Goldfinger's Silver Ghost is actually a Golden Ghost. Why?

8. What does Goldfinger do before he has his way with women?

9. Goldfinger captures Bond and lectures him on "pain" from the Latin *poena* meaning penalty. What penalty does he plan for our hero?

10. Who "invented" murder? And who was his brother, the first victim?

11. Bond is called St. George in tales including Goldfinger. What "saint" does Felix Leiter call him?

On Her Majesty's Secret Service Quiz

1. How does Bond sign his letters to M?

2. How often does Bond visit the little churchyard in Royale where a small granite cross is inscribed, "Vesper Lynd, R.I.P."?

3. What is the significance of the name Fleming gives to Marc-Ange Draco, head of an underworld organization and Tracy's father?

4. Marc-Ange offers Bond a million pounds. What is Bond's response?

5. What is Bond's family motto?

6. Blofeld transforms himself into a new body. What other evil figure also is characterized by such transformations?

7. What is the lethal substance in Blofeld's strategy for biological warfare that was lethally distributed in the U.S. in recent years?

8. Who is Bond's partner in the final assault on Blofeld's Swiss mountain compound?

9. Bond marries once. What happens to Tracy, his wife?

Dr. No, Live and Let Die and You Only Live Twice Quiz

<hr />

1. "You Only Live Twice" is the first line from a haiku patterned after Bassho, a Japanese poet. In the novel, to whom does Fleming ascribe the haiku?

2. The doctor's diagnosis of Bond, after the death of his wife, includes symptoms of shock, guilt, loss of zest for job and for life, excessive drinking and gambling. What is his spiritual diagnosis?

3. What does the doctor prescribe?

4. Who is Blofeld in his third incarnation?

5. Who takes up residence one-half mile across the water from Kissy's village? What do the villagers call the place and the owner?

6. What is the embellishment on Blofeld's silk kimono?

7. Who does Mr. Big's Voodoo cult believe him to be?

8. When we hear the line, "He disagreed with something that ate him," to whom does the line refer?

9. Like many of Bond's women, Honeychile Rider has a physical flaw. What's the flaw in her beautiful face?

10. What is the dragon in *Dr. No*?

11. What do Dr. No and President Millard Fillmore have in common?

12. What is M's full name?

Trivia Answers

General Trivia Answers

1. Chitty Chitty, Genii

2. Dr. No

3. Moneypenny, Loelia (Lil) Poinsby and Mary Goodnight

4. Q, Sir Arthur Quiller-Couch

5. Felix Leiter

6. George

7. Blofeld

8. Blofeld, *On Her Majesty's Secret Service*

9. *From Russia with Love*

10. Blofeld

Casino Royale Answers

1. The Vesper

2. Baccarat

3. SMERSH

4. Inverted M

5. Hoagy Carmichael

6. Right, right

7. Behind outer door plate

8. Devil

Diamonds Are Forever Answers

1. Gambling

2. True

3. Martinis

4. Studillac

5. Its aim is to trap the customer

6. Highland Light, an old 4-4-0 steam locomotive

7. Bovine blood; he is a bull

8. False

9. True

10. True

Moonraker Answers

1. May

2. Bentley coupe

3. It's a personal matter

4. 008, 0011

5. The letter S

6. Dragon

7. Culbertson hand

8. Pray (This tale lists at least five times he prays.)

9. Gala Brand

10. Pigeon

From Russia With Love **Answers**

1. Chief executioner for SMERSH

2. False

3. False

4. Rosa Klebb

5. Accidie

6. Bored

7. M's greed for a decoder; Bond's vanity and lust

8. Sewer

9. Orient Express

10. "Ours"

11. 10 pints

12. A miracle

Goldfinger Answers

1. Gold

2. Midas

3. Brooks Brothers suit

4. His Puritan heritage

5. *The Bible Designed to be Read as Literature*

6. St. Augustine

7. Body work is solid, 18-carat, white gold

8. Paints her body in gold

9. Run him through a table saw

10. Cain, Abel

11. St. James

On Her Majesty's Secret Service Answers

1. "I am, Sir, Your Obedient Servant"

2. Yearly

3. Angel

4. "I have enough money for my needs. I have my profession."

5. "The World Is Not Enough"

6. Devil

7. Anthrax

8. Marc-Ange

9. Murdered by Blofeld hours after their marriage

Dr. No, *Live and Let Die* and *You Only Live Twice* Answers

1. James Bond

2. Accidie

3. Something desperately important, but apparently impossible

4. Dr. Guntram Shatterhand

5. Devil, Hell, King of Death

6. A golden dragon

7. Baron Samedi

8. Felix Leiter

9. An uncorrected broken nose

10. A camouflaged tractor with a flame thrower

11. Guano or dung. Dr. No harvests guano to sell as fertilizer. President Fillmore noted the importance of Peruvian guano for U.S. agriculture in his 1850 State of the Union address.

12. Admiral Sir Miles Messervy

About the Author

Benjamin Pratt, whose Bond-age stretches over decades, has lectured on the mythological and theological nature of the Bond literary tales at the Smithsonian Institution, universities, churches and synagogues. He lives in Fairfax, Virginia.

Acknowledgments

Coincidence is a word laced throughout the Bond tales that assumes Bond's encounters with enemies and friends are more than an accident. For Ian Fleming, coincidence implies the intervention of God as an act of Providence.

It is with gratitude that I acknowledge the coincidence and Providence that brought the following people into my journey with James Bond.

It was certainly a coincidence that brought me together with David Crumm when I went to Ann Arbor a few years ago to teach about Henri Nouwen. Long after I had given up the idea of publishing my research on James Bond in book form, David remembered me and my 007 perspective. He approached me with the idea that I would write this new kind of book and, as my editor, he would help me to make it publication-worthy. I am deeply appreciative to David for taking my "piffle," as Fleming often referred to his tales, and making this very readable.

This book contains letters written by agents whose names need to remain private. What you read from these individuals will deepen your understanding and challenge your personal perspective. I deeply appreciate their responses.

My sincerest appreciation to close friends who have challenged, researched, probed and prodded and endured my time in Bond-age: Janice and Neal Gregory, Josie Jordan, Sharon Levy, Bill and Kara Sidener, Jim and Sandra Truxell. I am also grateful to the students who responded to my work with probing questions and enriching responses.

Last, and certainly not least, I acknowledge my deep appreciation for the love, support and encouragement from my immediate family. Judith, my wife of forty-five years has been a tireless friend and editor. Your love sustains me. Our two daughters and their families always offer support and love and helpful thoughts. Megan, Frank, Mary Stuart and Hannah Carter and Alexa, Dan, Maddie and Zachary Schaefer have my love and appreciation.

Colophon

This book was produced using methods that separate content from presentation. Doing so increases the flexibility and accessibility of the content and allows us to generate editions in varying presentation formats quickly and easily.

The content is stored in a standard XML format called DocBook 5 (www.DocBook.org). Adobe InDesign®, the Oxygen® XML Editor and Microsoft Word® were used in the production.

The print edition is set in Adobe Caslon Pro type with titles in Portago ITC Std.

Cover art and design by Rick Nease (www.RickNease.com)

Content editing by David Crumm (www.ReadTheSpirit.com)

Copy editing by Judith Pratt and Stephanie Fenton

Digital encoding and print layout by John Hile

Breinigsville, PA USA
08 September 2009
223679BV00001B/6/P